# BRIDGE HANDS
# TO MAKE YOU
# LAUGH . . . AND CRY

David Bird
and
Nikos Sarantakos

BATSFORD

First published 2004

© David Bird and Nikos Sarantakos 2004

The right of David Bird and Nikos Sarantakos to be identified as Authors of this work has been asserted by them in accordance with the Copyright, Designs and Patents Act 1988.

ISBN 0 7134 8896 4

A CIP catalogue record for this book is available from the British Library.

Typeset in the U.K. by Ruth Edmondson
Printed in the U.K. by Creative Print & Design, Ebbw Vale,Wales

for the publishers

B T Batsford, The Chrysalis Building, Bramley Road, London W10 6SP

An imprint of **Chrysalis** Books Group plc

Distributed in the United States and Canada by Sterling Publishing Co., 387 Park Avenue South, New York, NY 10016, USA

Editor: Elena Jeronimidis

# INTRODUCTION

The deals contained in this book have been gathered from far and wide – from the world's best bridge magazines, including England's *Bridge Magazine*, France's *Le Bridgeur* and USA's *Bridge World*, from world championship books and from various tournament bulletins. Some deals have been recounted to us by word of mouth. It would not be practical to name all the sources in the main text, since this would interfere with the reader's pleasure and the flow of the narrative. We pay homage here to the original reporters who witnessed such exceptional happenings and enriched the bridge world by sharing their experiences.

Some of the material in the book has appeared previously, under the sole authorship of Nikos, in England's *Bridge Plus* magazine.

A collection of deals such as this is similar to a programme of TV out-takes. The world's best players are sometimes seen at their worst, making mistakes of the sort that we ordinary players do. We hope they will accept such exposure, albeit with a rueful smile. Everyone knows that each atrocity these aces perform is hugely outnumbered by their clever plays and brilliancies. In any case, an embarrassingly weak defence produced by Emsley F. Wilderhorn of Palm Beach would not be newsworthy. If the great bridge public laps up an apparent error by a maestro such as Jeff Meckstroth, this is a compliment to his impeccable reputation and host of championship wins.

Enough of *apologia pro vita sua*. On with the entertainment!

*David Bird and Nikos Sarantakos*

# CONTENTS

# 1
# The Bald Man and the Fly

A surprising chapter heading in a bridge book, you may think. In fact it is the title of one of Aesop's fables. In an 1887 English translation, it reads:

*A Fly bit the bare head of a Bald Man who, endeavouring to destroy it, gave himself a heavy slap. Escaping, the Fly said mockingly, "You who have wished to revenge, even with death, the prick of a tiny insect, see what you have done to yourself to add insult to injury?"*

Similar situations arise at the bridge table. It sometimes happens that one side (the man, not necessarily bald) holds the great majority of points and is looking forward to a game, or possibly a slam. The other side (the fly) then makes an impertinent overcall on meagre values. Instead of brushing it aside and finding their contract, the point-laden pair decide to teach it a lesson (with a heavy double rather than slap). To add insult to injury, the tiny, low-level enemy contract makes!

Our first exhibit arose when Egypt faced USA in the 1968 Olympiad:

---

**Dealer: South. Love All.**

```
              ♠ 8 7 5 4
              ♡ Q 8
              ◇ Q J 5 3
              ♣ Q 8 5
♠ A 10 9 6                    ♠ —
♡ A 10            N           ♡ J 5 4 3
◇ 9 6 2      W       E        ◇ A K 10 4
♣ 9 7 6 4        S           ♣ A K J 10 3
              ♠ K Q J 3 2
              ♡ K 9 7 6 2
              ◇ 8 7
              ♣ 2
```

| West | North | East | South |
|------|-------|------|-------|
| *Mrs Morcos* | *Kay* | *Shaffei* | *Kaplan* |
| | | | Pass |
| Pass | Pass | 1♣ | 1♠ |
| Dbl | All Pass | | |

---

Negative doubles had not yet gained worldwide acceptance, so West's double was for penalties. What an awful call it was, particularly when holding four-card club support! Why try to make seven tricks with spades as trumps, with a known bad trump break against you, rather than attempting 1NT or a part-score in clubs? Mind you, her partner wasn't obliged to stand for it and might well have taken it out, given his spade void and attacking hand.

West led the ◊6 to the queen and king. East cashed the ♣A and then attempted to cash the king, which was fatal for the defence. Doubtless he couldn't believe that his partner would make a one-level penalty double with four-card club support. Declarer ruffed the second club and led a low heart. West rose with the ace and returned the ◊9, which held, and then another diamond, ruffed by declarer. The trump queen was allowed to win and Kaplan played a heart to the queen, followed by a second round of trumps to the jack and ace. West returned the ten of trumps to declarer's king. Kaplan then played the ♡K and claimed seven tricks.

At the other table the US pair were using negative doubles (in fact, Al Roth had invented them!) but they didn't have the chance to employ the method. The Egyptian South, a stunningly handsome amateur player who was surrounded by a swarm of kibitzers (you guessed it . . . Omar Sharif), made a take-out double instead of overcalling:

| West | North | East | South |
|------|-------|------|-------|
| Root | Zanariri | Roth | Sharif |
| | | | Pass |
| Pass | Pass | 1◊ | Dble |
| 1♠ | Pass | 2♣ | Pass |
| 3♣ | Pass | 5♣ | All Pass |

Al Roth and Bill Root bid efficiently to the club game (3NT was a sound alternative) and South led the ♠K to dummy's ace. Roth discarded a heart from hand and advanced the ◊9. North split his honours and in the fullness of time Roth was able to score eleven tricks even after misguessing the trumps. He lost just one heart and one trump. So, the insulting 160 was added to 400 and the Americans gained 11 IMPs.

Sometimes the fly can bite before the bald man – er . . . the strong hand – has had a chance to bid. This is what happened in the 2000 Maastricht Olympiad:

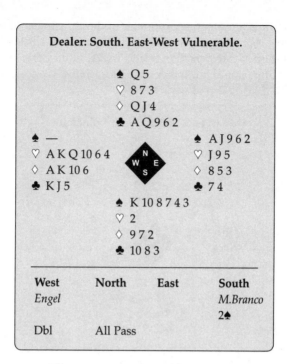

**Dealer: South. East-West Vulnerable.**

```
                    ♠ Q 5
                    ♡ 8 7 3
                    ◇ Q J 4
                    ♣ A Q 9 6 2
  ♠ —                                ♠ A J 9 6 2
  ♡ A K Q 10 6 4         N          ♡ J 9 5
  ◇ A K 10 6        W    E          ◇ 8 5 3
  ♣ K J 5                S          ♣ 7 4
                    ♠ K 10 8 7 4 3
                    ♡ 2
                    ◇ 9 7 2
                    ♣ 10 8 3
```

| West | North | East | South |
|------|-------|------|-------|
| *Engel* | | | *M.Branco* |
| | | | 2♠ |
| Dbl | All Pass | | |

The South hand may seem a bit light for a weak two bid, but at favourable vulnerability and first to speak Brazil's Marcelo Branco could not resist the temptation. Zvi Engel, West for Belgium, now had a real problem. Holding a game-forcing hand with a spade void, vulnerable against not, there was a real risk that a double might be passed out for an inadequate penalty. Engel did choose to double and partner passed it out. Who can blame him?

Insult was added to injury when Branco made his doubled contract. West began the defence with two top hearts. Branco ruffed the second round and advanced a low diamond, won by West. To beat the contract, it is essential to play hearts at every opportunity (East can then make an effective minor-suit discard on the fourth round of hearts). The Belgian West chose to shift to a low club at Trick 4 and in due time Branco collected eight tricks and +470.

Despite this triumph there was (naturally!) a fly in the ointment for Brazil. They gained only 9 IMPs because at the other table, given a free run, the Brazilian East-West over-reached to 6♡ and duly went down.

So far we have seen examples where the side that tries to swat the fly is able to make game, but prefers to double a lowly part-score only to see it make. What about a side having a slam available and doubling a lowly enemy contract unsuccessfully? This grotesque debacle has happened several times, even among well-known champions.

---

The first example arose in the semi-finals of the 1998 Spingold teams. At the first table, Jeff Meckstroth and Eric Rodwell bid efficiently to the good small slam in clubs, making twelve tricks. At the other table the fly put in a late appearance but it then stung forcefully:

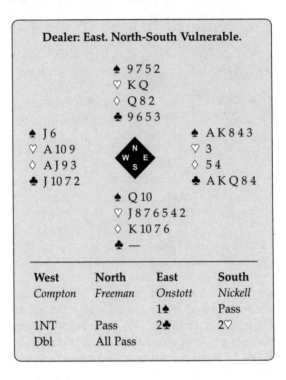

**Dealer: East. North-South Vulnerable.**

|  | ♠ 9 7 5 2 |  |
|---|---|---|
|  | ♡ K Q |  |
|  | ◇ Q 8 2 |  |
|  | ♣ 9 6 5 3 |  |
| ♠ J 6 |  | ♠ A K 8 4 3 |
| ♡ A 10 9 |  | ♡ 3 |
| ◇ A J 9 3 |  | ◇ 5 4 |
| ♣ J 10 7 2 |  | ♣ A K Q 8 4 |
|  | ♠ Q 10 |  |
|  | ♡ J 8 7 6 5 4 2 |  |
|  | ◇ K 10 7 6 |  |
|  | ♣ — |  |

| West | North | East | South |
|---|---|---|---|
| Compton | Freeman | Onstott | Nickell |
|  |  | 1♠ | Pass |
| 1NT | Pass | 2♣ | 2♡ |
| Dbl | All Pass |  |  |

East-West were playing a two-level response as game-forcing, so West began with a forcing 1NT response. We wonder what East would have needed to rebid 3♣. He chose a humble 2♣ rebid, which might have been made on a three-card suit, and the magnificent club fit never came to light.

That said, West's double of 2♡ was surely the main culprit. South knew he was bidding at unfavourable vulnerability and would not have stepped into the arena, on a passed hand, without considerable distributional values. West's trumps were simply not good enough to venture a penalty double, particularly when there were reasonable prospects of scoring a game in his own direction. There was no defence against 2♡ doubled and the Nickell squad picked up plus scores of 670 and 920, giving them an impressive 17 IMPs.

Fly-hitting accidents can happen even to the world's top players and our last example comes from the prestigious (but, alas, no longer with us) *Macallan* tournament of 1998. All four players at the table were among the world's elite:

```
                  Dealer: South. Love All.

                         ♠ K Q 6
                         ♡ K J 10 5 4 3
                         ♢ 10 9 8 2
                         ♣ —
      ♠ A J 9 7 5 2                      ♠ 10 3
      ♡ 9                  N             ♡ A Q 8 7 2
      ♢ A             W         E        ♢ K 4
      ♣ A Q 8 5 2          S            ♣ K J 6 4
                         ♠ 8 4
                         ♡ 6
                         ♢ Q J 7 6 5 3
                         ♣ 10 9 7 3
```

| West | North | East | South |
|------|-------|------|-------|
| *Robson* | *Helness* | *Zia* | *Helgemo* |
| | | | Pass |
| 1♠ | 2♡ | Pass | Pass |
| Dbl | Pass | Pass | 3♢ |
| Pass | Pass | Dbl | All Pass |

West's reopening double seemed to hit the jackpot for a moment or two. The Norwegian fly then rose into the air, seeking a more hospitable spot. The second double did not meet with success. Andrew Robson led his singleton heart to the ten and queen, and the defenders could not prevent declarer from disposing of his four club losers in one way or another.

How do we assign the blame here? West's re-opening double on the second round might well have picked up a big penalty against 2♡. However, it is always dangerous to conceal the second half of a big two-suiter. When you have a fit in the second suit, partner will over-estimate his defensive values and under-estimate how many tricks can be made by his own side. Here the big club fit never came to light and Zia Mahmood, uncertain what game might be makeable by East-West, chose to defend against 3♢.

Note that 3♢ can be beaten, but only on the difficult ♢A lead. West must then switch to clubs and East has to play the king of trumps if he comes in early with a heart.

A tiny (fly-weight) consolation for East-West was that not all pairs who reached 6♣ managed to make it. At the table of Lorenzo Lauria and Alfredo Versace, there was also a 2♡ overcall, but Alfredo Versace as West reopened with an excellent 4♣ bid instead of a double. The Italians soon found the good club slam and efficient bidding was followed by efficient play. Versace won the diamond lead and played a trump to the king. He led a second trump through South, who inserted the nine, and then played ace and another spade. He later ruffed a spade with the ♣J and finessed the ♣8 on the way back – 6♣ made.

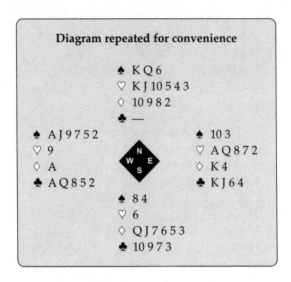

By contrast, Jeff Meckstroth, after winning the diamond lead, laid down the ace of trumps at Trick 2. A tiny difference, it seems, but now the slam could not be made! No longer able to ruff a spade high and pick up South's trumps, he went down.

The opponents had put in a fly-weight bid at Meckstroth's table and no doubt it was responsible for the slam's failure. Germany's Daniela von Arnim, sitting South, had opened with a weak 2◊. It therefore made sense for declarer to play South, rather than North, to be short in clubs. Yes, some flies can bite in devious ways!

# 2
# The World's Strongest Overcalls

W hat is the maximum strength for a simple overcall at the level of one or two? A few decades ago any hand of more than around 15 points would be launched with a take-out double. "My hand is far too strong for an overcall," players would say. "I'll start with a double and then bid my suit." Fashions change. Nowadays players are willing to risk a simple overcall on quite strong hands, sometimes on very strong hands.

In this chapter we will look at a few inordinately powerful simple overcalls. Eric Kokish, the Canadian expert, preaches that there is no such thing as a hand that is too strong for a simple overcall. You may wonder why such players do not sometimes miss game when they overcall on a giant hand. The main reason is that since the advent of negative doubles by the player sitting over the overcall, the opening bidder is likely to keep the auction alive after a start such as $1\diamond - 1\spadesuit - $ Pass $- $ Pass.

When a strong overcall is passed out, this is not necessarily a bad thing. The following deal arose in the match between Ireland and Switzerland in the 2000 European Junior Teams:

---

**Dealer: North. East-West Vulnerable.**

```
                    ♠ 6 3
                    ♡ 10 9 8 4
                    ◇ K 9 7 6 4
                    ♣ 5 4
   ♠ J 10 9 8 4              ♠ 2
   ♡ K 7 3 2          N      ♡ Q J 6 5
   ◇ —              W   E    ◇ A J 8 3 2
   ♣ J 8 6 2          S      ♣ K 10 3
                    ♠ A K Q 7 5
                    ♡ A
                    ◇ Q 10 5
                    ♣ A Q 9 7
```

| West | North | East | South |
|------|-------|------|-------|
|      |       |      | *Weisweiler* |
|      | Pass  | 1◇   | 1♠    |
| All Pass |   |      |       |

---

The Swiss South was presumably a fervent disciple of Eric Kokish. He opted for a mere 1♠ overcall, despite holding no fewer than 21 high-card points. With only one spade in their hand, many East players would have felt obligated to re-open with a double. That's because North could not raise the overcall and the odds are therefore high that West is waiting with a big trump stack.

No, the Irish East decided to let matters rest. John Weisweiler must have awaited the appearance of the dummy with some trepidation but eventually a lowly three-count was laid out. He made a comfortable eight tricks for 110, which was good for a small gain of 5 IMPs when at the other table the South player doubled the 1♢ opening bid and after the 1♡ response ended in 3NT minus two, a fate shared by the majority of the field. So, perhaps there is more than meets the eye to the Kokish approach of 'unlimited' overcalls.

When the strength lies in distributional values, rather than high-card points, the risk of an overcall being passed out is greatly minimized. If you have seven or eight hearts, for example, someone or other will surely mention spades and give you a second chance. The great Zia Mahmood relied on this theory when Pakistan met Indonesia in the qualifying rounds of the 1983 Bermuda Bowl. This was the deal:

**Dealer: West. North-South Vulnerable.**

```
                    ♠ K 10 8 3 2
                    ♡ —
                    ♢ A Q 5 4
                    ♣ 7 6 5 4
   ♠ 7                            ♠ Q 9 6 5
   ♡ 10 7 6 2          N          ♡ 8
   ♢ K 9 8 7 3 2    W   E         ♢ J 10
   ♣ 10 9              S          ♣ A K Q J 8 2
                    ♠ A J 4
                    ♡ A K Q J 9 5 4 3
                    ♢ 6
                    ♣ 3
```

| West | North | East | South |
|------|-------|------|-------|
| *Manoppo* | *Masood* | *Lasut* | *Zia* |
| Pass | Pass | 2♣ | 2♡ |
| Pass | 2♠ | Pass | 4NT |
| Pass | 5♢ | Pass | 6♡ |
| All Pass | | | |

East's 2♣ opening showed long clubs and around 10-15 points. What would you have bid on the South cards? Although Zia needed only the ♠Q opposite to make game, he contented himself with a 2♡ overcall. Was this risky? Not particularly, since he held only 15 points. The next question is: even if someone is likely to keep the bidding open, what do you gain by making such a modest bid? Zia's view was that by bidding 2♡ instead of 4♡ he was more likely to be able to judge if a slam was possible. His luck was in when Saleem Masood responded in spades. Out came the old Black and Zia was soon in 6♡.

A club was led, East winning with the jack. Zia ruffed the club continuation and drew trumps. Rather than take an immediate view on the two-way spade finesse, Zia decided to combine two chances. He first cashed ♠A and ♠K, which gave him a fair chance of dropping the queen. When the queen remained in hiding, he resorted to the second chance: a finesse of dummy's ◊Q. This chance paid off and the slam was made.

When the South players in other matches chose to overcall 4♡ the auction ended there. At one table South was not happy with any level of bid in hearts and started with a take-out double. His partner bid spades enthusiastically and ended in 5♠, going two down. So there is a lot to be said for Zia's 2♡ overcall – or shall we call it an 'undercall'?

The record for the strongest simple overcall does not belong to Zia. Fittingly, Eric Kokish has produced an even more extreme example, from the semi-finals of the 1985 Spingold:

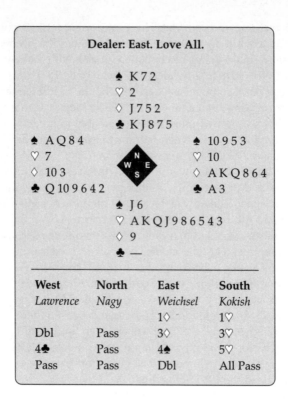

**Dealer: East. Love All.**

|  |  | ♠ K 7 2 |  |
|  |  | ♡ 2 |  |
|  |  | ◇ J 7 5 2 |  |
|  |  | ♣ K J 8 7 5 |  |

| ♠ A Q 8 4 |  |  | ♠ 10 9 5 3 |
| ♡ 7 |  |  | ♡ 10 |
| ◇ 10 3 |  |  | ◇ A K Q 8 6 4 |
| ♣ Q 10 9 6 4 2 |  |  | ♣ A 3 |

|  |  | ♠ J 6 |  |
|  |  | ♡ A K Q J 9 8 6 5 4 3 |  |
|  |  | ◇ 9 |  |
|  |  | ♣ — |  |

| West | North | East | South |
|------|-------|------|-------|
| *Lawrence* | *Nagy* | *Weichsel* | *Kokish* |
|  |  | 1◇ | 1♡ |
| Dbl | Pass | 3◇ | 3♡ |
| 4♣ | Pass | 4♠ | 5♡ |
| Pass | Pass | Dbl | All Pass |

What was Eric's purpose in bidding only 1♡ on his ten-card suit (a suit that most players will never be dealt in their lifetime)? It was different from Zia's on the previous deal. He hoped to buy the contract more easily at a higher level, on the basis that the opponents would think "He can't have that good a hand – he only bid 1♡ on it."

Well, that's how players might think at your local club, or in a 5p rubber game. World-class opponents such as Mike Lawrence and Peter Weichsel would not be taken in so lightly but it might still be difficult for them to judge exactly whose hand it was. Lawrence entered with a negative double and Weichsel chose to jump in diamonds, rather than bid his poor spade suit. Had the time come to bid 4♡? Not 'according to Kokish'! No, his values would be adequately covered by a 3♡ rebid. As Eric had judged, there was further bidding. His sandbagging tactics were vindicated when he eventually bought the contract at the five level and was doubled there. He made the contract easily, thanks to the precious ♠K that appeared in the dummy.

At the other table, Eric Rodwell was South and opted for an immediate 4♡ overcall. After a double from West and 4♠ from East, he went on to 5♡ and eventually sold out to 5♠. That was an unsatisfactory +50 for North-South and 12 IMPs to the Kokish squad.

In another match Ira Rubin bid even less than Kokish on the first round. When East opened 1◇ he passed on the South hand (this must also be a record of sorts). The auction then evolved in such a way that he later felt obliged to bid 6♡, which was one down. Ron Gerard fared better with an immediate 5♡ overcall, the contract being doubled and made. Summing up, Kaplan wrote in *Bridge World*: "I doubt that you can learn much in general about how to handle ten-card suits, but I find it satisfactory that the two successful actions were the credible underbid of one, and the bold leap to five."

Having thus established the records for super-strong overcalls at the minimum level, let's turn to another dimension. What is the record for the immediate highest overcall? The absolute record here would be 7NT and we confess that we don't have such an example. This deal, if you are willing to believe it, comes very close:

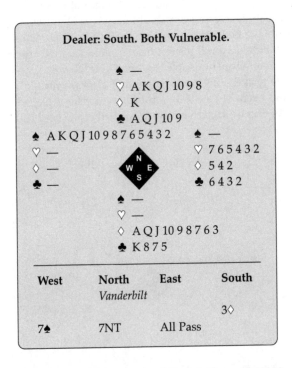

Dealer: South. Both Vulnerable.

|         | ♠ —           |          |       |
|         | ♡ A K Q J 10 9 8 |       |       |
|         | ◇ K           |          |       |
|         | ♣ A Q J 10 9  |          |       |

♠ A K Q J 10 9 8 7 6 5 4 3 2
♡ —
◇ —
♣ —

♠ —
♡ 7 6 5 4 3 2
◇ 5 4 2
♣ 6 4 3 2

♠ —
♡ —
◇ A Q J 10 9 8 7 6 3
♣ K 8 7 5

| West | North | East | South |
|------|-------|------|-------|
|      | *Vanderbilt* |       |       |
|      |       |      | 3◇    |
| 7♠   | 7NT   | All Pass |   |

The deal was reported to have occurred during the early 1930s at rubber bridge. A variant known as 'goulash' was being played where the unshuffled pack is dealt in packets of five, five and three cards around the table. This obviously makes for wild distributions but not to the extent that we should automatically believe that a real-life West was dealt a thirteen-card spade suit. (Amazing, isn't it, how many times a thirteen-card suit is claimed to be dealt and there are no matching claims of a twelve-card suit, even though this is many times more likely.)

South opened 3◊ which was natural and very strong in those days (it was game-forcing). West, who was not the world's leading expert in sandbagging, overcalled 7♠. He might been more circumspect if his thirteen-carder was in a lower suit than spades. Holding the senior suit, though, he could barely believe that he would be outbid. Sitting North was Harold Vanderbilt, the man who gave birth to contract bridge. He correctly inferred that West had to have all thirteen spades to bid this way after South's strong opening bid. He therefore bid 7NT. When the poor East player was unable to lead a spade, the grand rolled home, so Vanderbilt collected 2970 points under the scoring of the era (the grand slam bonus was 2250) instead of conceding 3110 for 7♠ doubled and made. The deal is included in Ely Culbertson's *Blue Book*. Culbertson adds that many players would have thought of bidding 7NT after having seen all four hands, but Mr Vanderbilt thought of it before.

You probably have as many doubts as we do about the veracity of the story, despite the Culbertson credentials. Still, as the Italians say, *se non è vero, è ben trovato*. (Even if it's not true, it makes a good story.)

If you prefer more verifiable examples you'll have to accept one notch lower as the record – an immediate grand slam overcall in hearts. In the Senior Teams event of the 1998 World Championships played in Lille, Karl Rohan of Austria was South on the first board of the very first match:

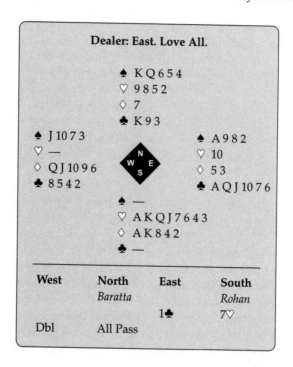

**Dealer: East. Love All.**

|  | North | | |
|---|---|---|---|
|  | ♠ K Q 6 5 4 | | |
|  | ♡ 9 8 5 2 | | |
|  | ◊ 7 | | |
|  | ♣ K 9 3 | | |

West
♠ J 10 7 3
♡ —
◊ Q J 10 9 6
♣ 8 5 4 2

East
♠ A 9 8 2
♡ 10
◊ 5 3
♣ A Q J 10 7 6

South
♠ —
♡ A K Q J 7 6 4 3
◊ A K 8 4 2
♣ —

| West | North | East | South |
|---|---|---|---|
|  | *Baratta* |  | *Rohan* |
|  |  | 1♣ | 7♡ |
| Dbl | All Pass | | |

East dealt and opened 1♣. Rohan had no conventional bid available to describe his 8-5 monster, so he bid what he hoped he could make, namely 7♡! West doubled, for some reason. Looking at his shape and lack of defensive values, one is tempted to believe that he was seeking the world record for the highest negative double ever made.

When Franz Baratta displayed four priceless trumps and a diamond singleton in the dummy the grand slam was laydown. At the other table South took a more scientific approach and the final contract was just 6♡. It was an auspicious hand for the Rohan team, who went on to win the Senior Teams world championship. More importantly, as we're sure you will agree, they gained a place in this book of ours!

# 3
# Front Page News

**R**ead all about it! The British pair bid and make 6♠, while at the other table the world's top player passes out 1♠! Did it ever really happen? No, but it very nearly did. The deal arose at the 1979 European Championships, which were contested in Lausanne, Switzerland:

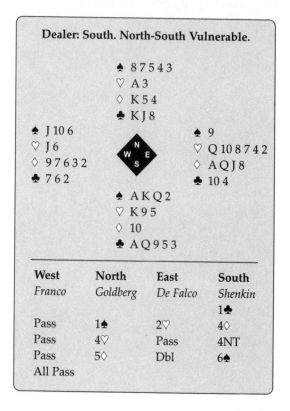

**Dealer: South. North-South Vulnerable.**

|  | ♠ 8 7 5 4 3 |  |
|---|---|---|
|  | ♡ A 3 |  |
|  | ◇ K 5 4 |  |
|  | ♣ K J 8 |  |
| ♠ J 10 6 |  | ♠ 9 |
| ♡ J 6 |  | ♡ Q 10 8 7 4 2 |
| ◇ 9 7 6 3 2 |  | ◇ A Q J 8 |
| ♣ 7 6 2 |  | ♣ 10 4 |
|  | ♠ A K Q 2 |  |
|  | ♡ K 9 5 |  |
|  | ◇ 10 |  |
|  | ♣ A Q 9 5 3 |  |

| West | North | East | South |
|---|---|---|---|
| *Franco* | *Goldberg* | *De Falco* | *Shenkin* |
|  |  |  | 1♣ |
| Pass | 1♠ | 2♡ | 4◇ |
| Pass | 4♡ | Pass | 4NT |
| Pass | 5◇ | Dbl | 6♠ |
| All Pass |  |  |  |

Barnet Shenkin's 4◇ rebid was a splinter bid, agreeing spades as trumps and showing at most one diamond. Dano De Falco doubled the 5◇ Blackwood response, to suggest a diamond lead, but Shenkin bid the small slam and had no problem in scoring twelve tricks.

At the other table this somewhat puzzling auction occurred:

| West | North | East | South |
|------|-------|------|-------|
| Priday | Garozzo | Rodrigue | Lauria |
| | | | 1♠ |
| Pass | Pass! | 2♡ | Pass |
| Pass | 4♠ | All Pass | |

Why did the great Benito Garozzo pass at his first turn? Screens were in use, with the bids relayed by an announcer. Garozzo heard "South: ONE SPADE, West: PASS," and in a rare moment of somnolence concluded that it was his right-hand opponent who had opened 1♠!

We asked the original West player, Tony Priday, about the incident. He recalled that at the end of the deal Lorenzo Lauria leaned forward to peer inquisitively through the gap in the screen. "What on earth happened?" he demanded, in Italian. An unruffled Garozzo waved the query dismissively aside.

# 4
# Grosvenor's Legacy

It is given to relatively few people to bequeath a lasting gift to the game of bridge. An undoubted member of this list is Philip Grosvenor, who invented a psychological manoeuvre known as the 'Grosvenor Coup', or 'Grosvenor Gambit'. It is performed by a defender when declarer is in a contract that is doomed to failure. By deliberately misdefending, he gives declarer a chance to succeed in his contract! Making the very reasonable assumption that the defender would not have defended in this way if it would allow the contract to make, declarer tumbles to defeat anyway. What does the performer of the coup gain by all this? He greatly annoys the declarer and openly expresses his disdain for him. (Yes, only very nasty players would indulge in a Grosvenor Coup.) The other benefit is that declarer is likely to play poorly for the next few hands.

That's enough of the theory. Let's see a real-life Grosvenor Coup, performed in 1961 by the great inventor himself. Indeed, it is the deal that originated the idea.

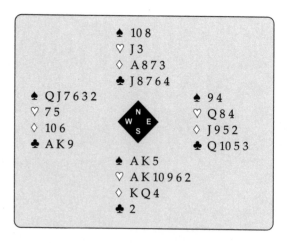

The hand, which was reported in USA's *Bridge World* magazine, was reconstructed by Frederick Turner of Los Angeles from notes that were discovered after Grosvenor's death. Grosvenor was sitting East, with two local experts occupying the North-South seats. The bidding was not given but South presumably opened with a demand bid because he later reached the ambitious contract of 6♡. Grosvenor's partner launched the defence with two top clubs and declarer ruffed the second round.

It was fairly obvious how to play the contract. Declarer cashed the two top spades and ruffed his remaining spade with dummy's ♡J. Grosvenor should have overruffed with the ♡Q, of course, putting the slam one down. Unfortunately he pulled a diamond from his hand and dummy's ♡J won the trick. Look at the deal from declarer's point of view now. He had been intending to finesse the ♡10 but East's failure to overruff in spades made it obvious that West held the ♡Q. Declarer therefore played to the drop the queen of trumps offside. When four low trumps appeared under his ace and king, declarer turned towards West conceding one down. "You make the queen of trumps," he said.

"I have the queen over here," declared Grosvenor.

The expert was so shell-shocked by the experience that he revoked on the next board and ended the session with a 41% score. Although Grosvenor had achieved the coup accidentally, he began to think that it might be worthwhile to attempt such psychological moves deliberately. A new field of play had been added to our great game!

Frederick Turner's article in *Bridge World* went on to document several other Grosvenor Coups performed by the great man during the 1960s. He concluded his narrative with this text:

*The rest is common knowledge, of course. Three days after this tournament Grosvenor's body was found on the beach at Key Largo. The dealing fingers of his right hand had been broken, and there were cruel bruises about his head and shoulders. In spite of the note found in his room at the Golden Whelk Motel and the coroner's subsequent ruling of suicide, there are those who still question the circumstances of Grosvenor's death.*

Turner's article, it transpired, was pure fantasy from beginning to end. It was written so convincingly, however, that many accepted it as fact. American Ace, John Swanson, tells the story of how Turner sent a copy of his article to a close friend, a member of The American Board of Nuclear Medicine. He received the following reply:

*I am enthralled by your letter relative to the Grosvenor Gambit. I confess I know so little about bridge that I hope sometime you will explain to me why it so infuriated some of the people who had it pulled on them. I certainly can't see how that could justify murdering a man! Neither can I understand from what you tell me about the findings on this man's corpse that the coroner could find it as a case of suicide! It shows that coroners are frail and probably susceptible to pressure and other unfortunate attributes of the human species.*

Turner, not wishing to embarrass his friend, never told him the truth.

So, it seems that our first deal never really occurred. Never mind, it will give you a general flavour of what the Grosvenor Coup is all about. Let's return to the real world. In the 1997 NABC played in Albuquerque the *New York Times* correspondent, Alan Truscott, fell victim to the coup. This was the deal:

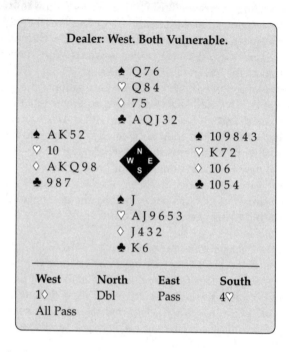

Dealer: West. Both Vulnerable.

|   | ♠ Q 7 6 |   |
|---|---------|---|
|   | ♡ Q 8 4 |   |
|   | ◇ 7 5 |   |
|   | ♣ A Q J 3 2 |   |
| ♠ A K 5 2 | | ♠ 10 9 8 4 3 |
| ♡ 10 | | ♡ K 7 2 |
| ◇ A K Q 9 8 | | ◇ 10 6 |
| ♣ 9 8 7 | | ♣ 10 5 4 |
|   | ♠ J |   |
|   | ♡ A J 9 6 5 3 |   |
|   | ◇ J 4 3 2 |   |
|   | ♣ K 6 |   |

| West | North | East | South |
|------|-------|------|-------|
| 1◇ | Dbl | Pass | 4♡ |
| All Pass | | | |

West led the ◇K against Truscott's heart game. He was following the modern style of leads known as 'ace for attitude, king for count', where you lead the king from an A-K combination when you want partner to give you a count signal rather than an attitude signal. East duly signalled with the ◇10, showing an even number of diamonds.

West's next move was to lead the ♠K. This time East played the ♠3 to indicate an odd number of cards in the suit. When the ♠J fell from declarer, the odds were high from West's point of view that East held five spades to South's one. At Trick 3, West continued with the ◇A, his partner playing the ◇6. Could West tell if his partner held two diamonds rather than four? Yes. From a four-card holding you should signal with the second card followed by the fourth. Most of the time, this will remove any ambiguity in the situation. Here, for example, East's ◇6 couldn't possibly be his fourth-best diamond, so West would know that East held a doubleton diamond (whatever confusing cards declarer may have chosen to play).

West could have beaten the contract by playing a third round of diamonds. East would have been able to overruff the dummy with the ♡K and that would be one down. Whether he knew what he was doing will never be known, but West decided to continue with the ♠A. Truscott ruffed in the South hand and could now have made the contract by crossing to the ♣J and leading the ♡Q, picking up the trump suit. (He would later overtake the ♣K with the ace and take two discards on the ♣Q and the ♠Q even if the clubs were not 3-3.) However, Truscott asked himself: "Why didn't West play a third round of diamonds?" His conclusion was that West must hold the bare ♡K and be nervous of exposing the situation. Had he led a third diamond in that case and East had been unable to overruff dummy's ♡Q, it would have been obvious that West held the ♡K.

You will have guessed by now what happened. Truscott laid down the ♡A, hoping to drop a singleton king from West. No red monarch appeared and the game was one down. Chalk up another victim to the Grosvenor Coup, although there is no reason to think that the perpetrator acted through clear design.

At the 2000 NABC, contested in Anaheim, David Treadwell was the victim of a similar coup. The deal arose during a Spingold match.

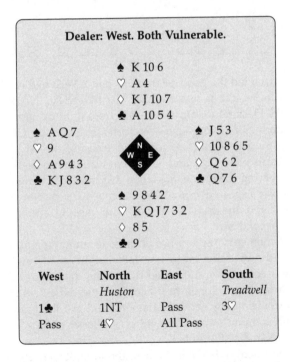

**Dealer: West. Both Vulnerable.**

|  | ♠ K 10 6 |  |
|---|---|---|
|  | ♡ A 4 |  |
|  | ◇ K J 10 7 |  |
|  | ♣ A 10 5 4 |  |
| ♠ A Q 7 | | ♠ J 5 3 |
| ♡ 9 | | ♡ 10 8 6 5 |
| ◇ A 9 4 3 | | ◇ Q 6 2 |
| ♣ K J 8 3 2 | | ♣ Q 7 6 |
|  | ♠ 9 8 4 2 |  |
|  | ♡ K Q J 7 3 2 |  |
|  | ◇ 8 5 |  |
|  | ♣ 9 |  |

| West | North | East | South |
|---|---|---|---|
|  | *Huston* |  | *Treadwell* |
| 1♣ | 1NT | Pass | 3♡ |
| Pass | 4♡ | All Pass |  |

Treadwell's 3♡ response was described as 'invitational with a six-card suit'. Since North held only two hearts and a minimum count for his 1NT overcall, he was pushing it a bit to raise to game. No doubt he made some allowance for the prime honour cards and the three ten-spots.

West led a low club and Treadwell rose with dummy's ace. After drawing trumps in four rounds, he led a spade towards dummy. West rose with the ace and led another club, ruffed by declarer. A spade to the king and a third round of the suit, won by West's queen, revealed the 3-3 spade break. West persisted with clubs, removing declarer's last trump, and this position had been reached:

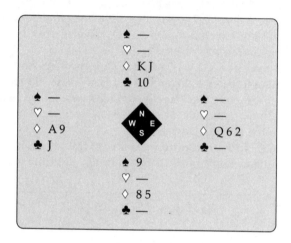

When Treadwell led the good ♠9 from his hand, West had only to throw the ◊9 and he would have scored the last two tricks. No, he chose to throw the ♣J! Declarer discarded the ♣10 from dummy and would now make his contract if he could guess correctly in diamonds. Of course, the only explanation he could see for West releasing the ♣J was that his remaining cards were ◊Q-x and he did not want to expose the diamond position by baring the queen. So, when declarer led a diamond at Trick 12 and the ◊9 appeared from West, he called for dummy's jack. The defenders scored the last two tricks, with the ◊Q and ◊A, and the contract was one down.

At such moments declarer needs an understanding partner. Michael Huston, North, was reported to have fallen off his chair laughing!

(Declarer could have succeeded by playing to his king of trumps at Trick 2 and leading a spade to the king. If the defenders persist with clubs, he can eventually set up a diamond and ruff the fourth round of spades with dummy's ace. That will give him seven trump tricks and three winners in the side suits.)

The next board was the sixtieth in the final of the 1998 Australian National Championship. It was not the perfect setting for a Grosvenor Coup because it was near the end of the 64-board match and the victim would therefore suffer any after-effects for only four more boards. However . . .

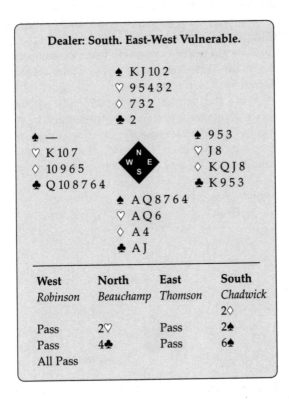

Dealer: South. East-West Vulnerable.

```
                        ♠ K J 10 2
                        ♡ 9 5 4 3 2
                        ◇ 7 3 2
                        ♣ 2
        ♠ —                             ♠ 9 5 3
        ♡ K 10 7              N         ♡ J 8
        ◇ 10 9 6 5       W        E     ◇ K Q J 8
        ♣ Q 10 8 7 6 4       S         ♣ K 9 5 3
                        ♠ A Q 8 7 6 4
                        ♡ A Q 6
                        ◇ A 4
                        ♣ A J
```

| West | North | East | South |
|------|-------|------|-------|
| *Robinson* | *Beauchamp* | *Thomson* | *Chadwick* |
| | | | 2◇ |
| Pass | 2♡ | Pass | 2♠ |
| Pass | 4♣ | Pass | 6♠ |
| All Pass | | | |

South's 2◇ showed a strong hand and 2♡ was a negative response. North's leap to 4♣ was a splinter bid, agreeing spades as trumps and showing at most one club. Ian Robinson led the ♣7 against the resultant slam and Ted Chadwick captured East's king with the ace. When he played the ace of trumps, the 3-0 break was revealed.

Declarer now had to set up the hearts for one loser and then discard his diamond loser on a good heart. It seems best to finesse the ♡Q but Chadwick decided to cash the ♡A at Trick 3. On this trick Ian Robinson, West, followed with the ♡10! His method, in general, was to play reverse-count discards. Of course, you should never waste a potentially useful card just to signal, and here the ♡10 had given declarer a chance to make a previously impossible contract. Declarer could now have drawn trumps in two more rounds and played a heart to the jack and queen. It would not help West to hold up the ♡K because declarer could clear the suit and there would still be an entry to dummy (the club ruff).

Very fortunately for West, Chadwick could not afford to follow this line. Suppose he drew two more rounds of trumps and led a heart towards his hand, East having started with ♡K-J-x. East would rise with the king, blocking the heart suit, and then play another round of clubs to kill the last entry to dummy! Realising this, Chadwick crossed to dummy with a second round of trumps and then led another heart while there was still a trump out. This went to the jack, queen and king and West delivered a heart ruff to beat the contract. Again we will need something approaching a sworn statement from 'Down Under' before we accept that West's Grosvenor Coup was intended.

We are nearing the end of the chapter and, amazingly, all our Grosvenor Coups so far seem to have been performed by mistake. Let's rectify matters with a deliberate example performed by one of the world's top players. Step forward Norway's Geir Helgemo, who was competing in the 1998 Cavendish, a big-money event for invited experts only.

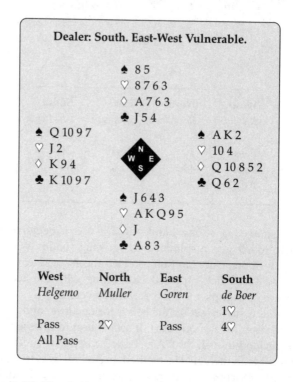

**Dealer: South. East-West Vulnerable.**

|  | ♠ 8 5 |  |
|---|---|---|
|  | ♡ 8 7 6 3 |  |
|  | ◊ A 7 6 3 |  |
|  | ♣ J 5 4 |  |
| ♠ Q 10 9 7 |  | ♠ A K 2 |
| ♡ J 2 |  | ♡ 10 4 |
| ◊ K 9 4 |  | ◊ Q 10 8 5 2 |
| ♣ K 10 9 7 |  | ♣ Q 6 2 |
|  | ♠ J 6 4 3 |  |
|  | ♡ A K Q 9 5 |  |
|  | ◊ J |  |
|  | ♣ A 8 3 |  |

| West | North | East | South |
|---|---|---|---|
| *Helgemo* | *Muller* | *Goren* | *de Boer* |
|  |  |  | 1♡ |
| Pass | 2♡ | Pass | 4♡ |
| All Pass |  |  |  |

As we see it, Wubbo de Boer was worth only a game-try bid of 2♠ at his second turn. His partner would probably then have signed off in 3♡, despite the favourable spade holding. Macho experts don't like to admit uncertainty by making game tries, however, and de Boer leapt all the way to 4♡ – a truly awful contract. (In Britain a bid such as South's 4♡ is known as a 'Landy game-try', after the former world champion, Sandra Landy, who favours such a direct bidding style. You bid game all by yourself and then try to make it!)

When Helgemo led the ♣10, Barry Goren won with the king and switched to a diamond, driving out dummy's ace. After ruffing one diamond in his hand, de Boer conceded a second spade trick. Goren won with the ace and switched to a trump. Declarer won with the ace, ruffed a spade, returned to the ♡K and ruffed his last spade. A diamond ruff to his hand left this end position:

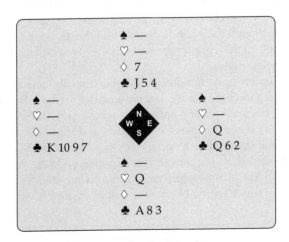

From declarer's point of view the contract was not yet dead. The spades and diamonds had been eliminated from West's hand. If he was down to ♣K-Q-x-x a low club towards the jack would end-play him. With this hope in mind, and his fingers crossed for good luck, Wubbo de Boer led the ♣3 towards dummy.

Helgemo knew the exact position at this stage. (Andrew Robson, a frequent team-mate, considers that Helgemo is the quickest player in the world to 'see' a hand – in other words to realise the key point that will be encountered.) He could easily have played low, allowing East to win with the ♣Q and exit safely in either minor. Did he do this? No, because there was a whiff of a Grosvenor Coup in the air.

For a moment, Helgemo raised declarer's hopes by rising with the ♣K. Did the Norwegian now exit with the ♣10, dooming the contract? No, he led an artistic ♣7. Declarer could then have made the contract by running the ♣7 to his ♣8, forcing East's ♣Q. Naturally he could not believe that one of the world's top players had presented him with such a chance, nor that Helgemo would have put up the ♣K unless he also held the queen. "Play the jack," he said. East covered with the queen and the game was one down, as Nature had always intended.

# 5
# You Overcalled on That Rubbish?

"An overcall, unlike an opening bid, should be based on a good suit. One of the purposes of making such a bid is to attract an advantageous opening lead." Sound words, yes, and the like of them can be found in countless books on bidding. However, many top-class players cannot resist the urge to enter the auction, even though their hands do not fulfil the textbook requirements for an overcall. In this chapter we will admire, or castigate, some of the more extreme examples.

Edgar Kaplan once famously said that the difference between a brave bid and a foolhardy one is largely a matter of result. By this token, some of the overcalls in our anthology were brave (they produced a positive result), while others were foolhardy and led to disaster.

The general standard for a one-level overcall is around 8-16 points and a good suit, headed by at least a couple of honours. On the very first deal of the 1958 World Championship match between Italy and North America, Pietro Forquet struck with a 1♠ overcall despite holding a very weak suit:

---

**Dealer: South. Both Vulnerable.**

```
                    ♠ A Q 9 4 2
                    ♡ 10 7 3
                    ◇ J 7 6
                    ♣ J 9

  ♠ 10 7 6 5 3              ♠ J 8
  ♡ K Q 8         N         ♡ J
  ◇ K Q        W     E      ◇ 10 9 5 4 2
  ♣ 10 8 3         S         ♣ A 7 6 5 2

                    ♠ K
                    ♡ A 9 6 5 4 2
                    ◇ A 8 3
                    ♣ K Q 4
```

| West | North | East | South |
|------|-------|------|-------|
| *Forquet* | *Roth* | *Siniscalco* | *Stone* |
| | | | 1♡ |
| 1♠ | Dbl | 2♣ | 2♠ |
| Pass | 3♡ | Pass | 4♡ |
| All Pass | | | |

---

Alvin Roth was the inventor of the negative double, but at this moment of history his double was for penalties. What do you make of Guglielmo Siniscalco's decision to run to 2♣? If you witnessed such a bid in a club game nowadays, you would shake your head. With J-x of trumps, a side-suit ace and a ruffing value in hearts, why not pass? There is no guarantee of a club fit and you will be a level higher. (Terence Reese once made the valuable observation that to fare better one level higher, you have to score two tricks more.) Apart from that, if you don't fancy your prospects in 1♠, it is better to make an SOS redouble to ask partner to choose between your five-card minors. A redouble must have meant something different in those days.

Tobias Stone arrived eventually in 4♡, which was easily defeated after the ◊K lead. Declarer lost one diamond, one club and two trumps, going one down. At the other table John Crawford, West for North America, did not overcall. Eugenio Chiaradia made an overtrick in 2♡ and gained 3 IMPs, according to the less generous scale then in use. Using the Kaplan yardstick, the Forquet overcall was 'brave' especially since he was vulnerable and penalty doubles were in use.

Forquet overcalled on an anaemic suit, admittedly, but he did at least hold 10 points. Let's see an example of an overcall on a weaker hand, albeit with a stronger suit. It occurred in the 1991 Bermuda Bowl played in Yokohama, when the home team met the reigning European champions, Great Britain:

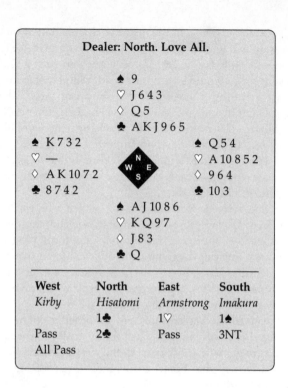

**Dealer: North. Love All.**

|             |           |              | ♠ 9          |
|             |           |              | ♡ J 6 4 3    |
|             |           |              | ◇ Q 5        |
|             |           |              | ♣ A K J 9 6 5 |

♠ K 7 3 2          ♠ Q 5 4
♡ —                ♡ A 10 8 5 2
◇ A K 10 7 2       ◇ 9 6 4
♣ 8 7 4 2          ♣ 10 3

|             |           |              | ♠ A J 10 8 6 |
|             |           |              | ♡ K Q 9 7    |
|             |           |              | ◇ J 8 3      |
|             |           |              | ♣ Q          |

| West | North | East | South |
|------|-------|------|-------|
| *Kirby* | *Hisatomi* | *Armstrong* | *Imakura* |
|  | 1♣ | 1♡ | 1♠ |
| Pass | 2♣ | Pass | 3NT |
| All Pass | | | |

Seeking to gain an advantage on the first board of the match, John Armstrong ventured an overcall on the somewhat unimpressive East hand. When no spade fit emerged, Tadashi Imakura looked no further than the obvious 3NT. Graham Kirby was spared the familiar "Do I lead my suit or his?" decision, since he was void in hearts. He led a diamond and the contract was one down when Armstrong pounced on the first round of hearts, returning a diamond.

In the other room, Sowter-Smolski reached an uncontested 4♡, played by South. With hearts 5-0, you might expect the contract to fail miserably – an indirect punishment of Armstrong's overcall in the other room. However, 4♡ was made. West cashed two top diamonds and switched to a spade, drawing the queen and ace. Roman Smolski played the ♡K, ducked, and then cashed ◇J and ♣Q. After ruffing a spade, he played good clubs through East. What could East do? He discarded his last spade on the third club and ruffed the fourth; Smolski overruffed and ruffed his last spade with the jack. That was +420 and 10 IMPs to Great Britain. If East ruffs earlier, Smolski would be able to ruff another spade low and come to a similar position. All in all, Armstrong's overcall led to a sizeable gain, so it was indisputably a brave bid.

In our next example the suit overcalled is slightly weaker and the hand contains one point fewer – a mere five points. The proud overcaller was multiple world champion, Jeff Meckstroth. Actually, this effort comes from his very first (and successful) attempt at the world crown. It was the 1981 Bermuda Bowl final between Pakistan and USA:

```
Dealer: East. North-South Vulnerable.

                    ♠ K 8 2
                    ♡ J 4
                    ◊ A 9
                    ♣ K Q 9 8 5 4
  ♠ J 7                              ♠ 10 9 5 4
  ♡ A 10 6 5 3          N           ♡ K Q 8
  ◊ 7 5 3 2         W       E       ◊ Q J 10 4
  ♣ 6 3                 S           ♣ J 7
                    ♠ A Q 6 3
                    ♡ 9 7 2
                    ◊ K 8 6
                    ♣ A 10 2
```

| West | North | East | South |
|------|-------|------|-------|
| *Meckstroth* | *Munir* | *Rodwell* | *Fazli* |
| | | Pass | 1♣ |
| 1♡ | 2♡ | 3♡ | 3♠ |
| Pass | 4♣ | Pass | 5♣ |
| All Pass | | | |

This was Board 2 of the final. It's interesting that the two previous examples were also played at the very beginning of the match. You must judge whether it was a coincidence. Perhaps the great champions make dubious overcalls at the start of a match to assert their authority and to serve notice that they are active bidders. Whether or not there is any truth in this, Jeff Meckstroth deemed his hand worthy of a 1♡ overcall. This time the macho tactic assisted the opponents. The Pakistanis were not playing inverted minor raises and North would have had to manufacture some bid, had West not intervened. After an overcall it was easy to show his hand with a cue-bid and Jan-E-Alam Fazli was soon in the admirable contract of 5♣, which was easily made.

At other table, without the intervention, the American North raised to 2♣ (an inverted minor raise). The auction continued 2NT – 3NT and a heart lead gave the defenders the first five tricks, Pakistan gaining 12 IMPs. Kaplan would surely have assessed Meckstroth's 1♡ as a reckless overcall, fully deserving an adverse swing!

In case you are not satisfied with the fare so far provided, let us proceed to real extremes. Assuming that an overcall promises at least a five-card suit (we will see in Chapter 10 some corner-cutting as to suit length), the absolutely worst suit you could hold is 6-5-4-3-2. We blushingly admit we don't have such a gem in our collection. Will one notch higher do – an overcall on a seven-high suit? The deal wasn't particularly noteworthy but the perpetrator was vulnerable and, yes, he was yet another world champion! Italy faced USA for the 1957 Bermuda Bowl:

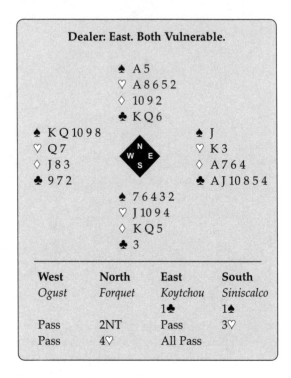

### Dealer: East. Both Vulnerable.

|  | ♠ A 5 |  |
|---|---|---|
|  | ♡ A 8 6 5 2 |  |
|  | ◇ 10 9 2 |  |
|  | ♣ K Q 6 |  |
| ♠ K Q 10 9 8 |  | ♠ J |
| ♡ Q 7 |  | ♡ K 3 |
| ◇ J 8 3 |  | ◇ A 7 6 4 |
| ♣ 9 7 2 |  | ♣ A J 10 8 5 4 |
|  | ♠ 7 6 4 3 2 |  |
|  | ♡ J 10 9 4 |  |
|  | ◇ K Q 5 |  |
|  | ♣ 3 |  |

| West | North | East | South |
|---|---|---|---|
| Ogust | Forquet | Koytchou | Siniscalco |
|  |  | 1♣ | 1♠ |
| Pass | 2NT | Pass | 3♡ |
| Pass | 4♡ | All Pass |  |

Guglielmo Siniscalco overcalled on a 7-high suit and a 6-point hand. He was vulnerable, too! A beginner making such a bid would attract a few strange looks and indeed it is hard to divine what purpose the Italian had in mind. Unfortunately for him, partner was strong and drove to game, which had to go one down. At the other table Helen Sobel made 3♡ exactly, played by North, and the US won 240 total points.

What is the weakest hand ever to make an overcall in term of high-card points? Here again, we grudgingly admit that our anthology does not contain any examples of zero-point overcalls made at world championship level. Perhaps you will bear with us while we show you two where the overcaller had just one point, a humble jack, in his hand.

The first case happened during the 1976 Olympiad in Monte Carlo:

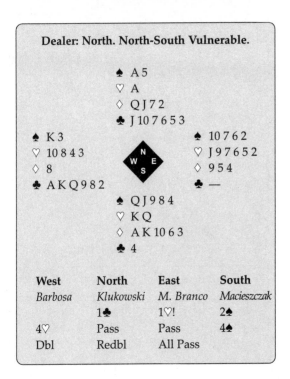

**Dealer: North. North-South Vulnerable.**

```
              ♠ A 5
              ♡ A
              ◊ Q J 7 2
              ♣ J 10 7 6 5 3
♠ K 3                         ♠ 10 7 6 2
♡ 10 8 4 3          N         ♡ J 9 7 6 5 2
◊ 8              W     E       ◊ 9 5 4
♣ A K Q 9 8 2       S         ♣ —
              ♠ Q J 9 8 4
              ♡ K Q
              ◊ A K 10 6 3
              ♣ 4
```

| West | North | East | South |
|------|-------|------|-------|
| *Barbosa* | *Klukowski* | *M. Branco* | *Macieszczak* |
| | 1♣ | 1♡! | 2♠ |
| 4♡ | Pass | Pass | 4♠ |
| Dbl | Redbl | All Pass | |

Second-position overcalls tend to be a tad stronger than in the third or fourth position, when partner has passed. Marcelo Branco threw caution to the winds with a merry 1♡ overcall on a jack-high suit. ("When I was young I sometimes made bids like this," he replied, when Nikos sent him an e-mail about the hand.)

One might think that he got what he deserved when 4♠ was doubled and redoubled, the Polish declarer making ten tricks for +1030. (There is no defence to eleven tricks, as it happens, since East has no clubs with which to force the South hand.) No, the guardian angels sitting North-South for Brazil at the other table came to the rescue. Gabriel Chagas and Pedro PauloAssumpçao reached and made the excellent small slam in diamonds, scoring +1370. The 1♡ overcall was therefore a brave effort.

In the 2002 Rosenblum Cup final, with Italy facing Indonesia, Branco's record was tied by another world champion, Alfredo Versace. He held a similar heart suit in an equally weak hand. There was perhaps less risk in his light overcall because his partner had already passed.

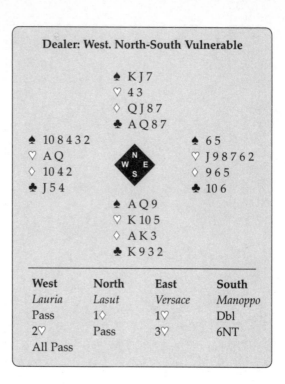

**Dealer: West. North-South Vulnerable**

```
                    ♠ K J 7
                    ♡ 4 3
                    ◊ Q J 8 7
                    ♣ A Q 8 7
    ♠ 10 8 4 3 2              ♠ 6 5
    ♡ A Q                     ♡ J 9 8 7 6 2
    ◊ 10 4 2                  ◊ 9 6 5
    ♣ J 5 4                   ♣ 10 6
                    ♠ A Q 9
                    ♡ K 10 5
                    ◊ A K 3
                    ♣ K 9 3 2
```

| West | North | East | South |
|------|-------|------|-------|
| *Lauria* | *Lasut* | *Versace* | *Manoppo* |
| Pass | 1◊ | 1♡ | Dbl |
| 2♡ | Pass | 3♡ | 6NT |
| All Pass | | | |

Lorenzo Lauria would probably have led the ♡A-Q against 3NT. It was a different matter against 6NT. He led a passive spade and declarer had no option but to lead towards the ♡K for his twelfth trick. No cameraman was present to record Eddy Manoppo's expression as his king lost to the ace, so we will have to use our imagination. Once again the perpetrator of a seemingly purposeless overcall on rubbish had emerged smelling of roses.

In the other room the East player, Karwur for Indonesia also overcalled, but he used a pre-emptive jump overcall of 3♡, a more orthodox action. Despite the pre-empt, Norberto Bocchi and Giorgio Duboin gauged the deal accurately, applying the brakes at 4NT. Italy gained 13 IMPs on the board and went on to win the match and the trophy.

It seems that this East hand has a strange appeal because neither man nor machine can resist the urge to bid when holding it. When Nikos replayed this deal with GIB, Matt Ginsberg's excellent (albeit idiosyncratic) bridge-playing computer program, the East 'player' also saw fit to overcall, choosing a weak 2♡. South immediately jumped to 6NT (GIB doesn't beat around the bush). The GIB West then led . . . the ♡A! What is the moral of this little tale? Both humans and computers overcall on tram tickets but computers trust their silicon partners more than humans do!

*Bridge Hands to Make You Laugh . . . and Cry*

# 6
# Nine Down in Four Spades

With ♠A-K-Q-J-10-3-2 in your hand you would not be surprised to hear that the final contract was 4♠. Perhaps you might be, though, if you were told that it was the opponents who were in the spade game. The situation arose in the 2003 Pacific Asia championships and was reported by Brian Senior. New Zealand faced Indonesia in the Seniors event:

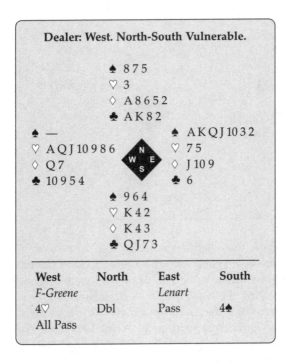

Dealer: West. North-South Vulnerable.

```
              ♠ 875
              ♡ 3
              ◊ A8652
              ♣ AK82
♠ —                      ♠ AKQJ10 3 2
♡ AQJ10986               ♡ 75
◊ Q7                     ◊ J109
♣ 10954                  ♣ 6
              ♠ 964
              ♡ K42
              ◊ K43
              ♣ QJ73
```

| West | North | East | South |
|------|-------|------|-------|
| *F-Greene* | | *Lenart* | |
| 4♡ | Dbl | Pass | 4♠ |
| All Pass | | | |

The Indonesian North entered with a take-out double and Tony Lenart passed on the East cards, awaiting developments. Suppose you had been South. What action would you have taken? It is surely best to pass the double, hoping to score at least four tricks in defence. No, South expected his partner to hold the other major strongly and opted for the spade game.

When Robyn Freeman-Greene led the ♣10, declarer won in dummy and played a heart, hoping to score a ruff or two. This hope was dispelled when West won and played another club. Lenart ruffed in the East seat and proceeded to draw trumps. He then returned a heart, allowing the defenders to score the balance.

That was nine down for the unusual score of +900. At the other table 4♡ was defeated for a 14-IMP gain. After taking their three minor-suit winners, the defenders forced the dummy with a second round of clubs to prevent declarer running the ♡7 for a repeated finesse.

Suppose that East had bid 4♠ at the second table, perhaps setting an unusual record for the highest identical contract played by pairs of the same team. How do you think he would have fared?

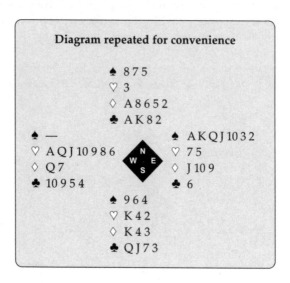

**Diagram repeated for convenience**

```
                    ♠ 8 7 5
                    ♡ 3
                    ◇ A 8 6 5 2
                    ♣ A K 8 2
    ♠ —                             ♠ A K Q J 10 3 2
    ♡ A Q J 10 9 8 6      N         ♡ 7 5
    ◇ Q 7             W     E       ◇ J 10 9
    ♣ 10 9 5 4           S          ♣ 6
                    ♠ 9 6 4
                    ♡ K 4 2
                    ◇ K 4 3
                    ♣ Q J 7 3
```

To beat the game the defenders must arrange a heart ruff. A low heart lead from South is not good enough because declarer can run the lead to his seven. He will then be able to draw trumps and score all thirteen tricks by repeating the heart finesse. A double-dummy lead of the ♡K would succeed, since declarer would have to win in the dummy and would have no quick entry to his hand. A club lead is no good, of course, because it sets up a ruffing route to declarer's hand. The best practical chance of defeating the spade game is for South to lead a diamond. North would win with the ace and should then switch to his singleton heart. South covers declarer's ♡7 with the king and a heart ruff would soon follow.

# 7
# Horrible Defences at Trick 2

They say that blind opening leads are for deaf players only. It's a bit of an exaggeration and the opening lead is often made pretty much in the dark. If you choose the wrong opening lead the chances are that your partner will at least pretend to be sympathetic.

What about Trick 2, though? Having seen the first trick and the thirteen cards in the dummy, a defender will have much less excuse for going astray. In this chapter we will see some of the world's top players making very much the wrong move on the second trick. Chuckle briefly if you must but our main purpose will be to analyse whether the defender should have done better.

In the 1972 Olympiad France just edged out Chinese Taipei for the fourth semi-final berth. In the match between these two teams Chinese Taipei won 15-5, though, and this deal helped:

---

**Dealer: East. North-South Vulnerable.**

```
                    ♠ J 10 6
                    ♡ K 9 4 2
                    ◊ 8
                    ♣ A J 10 5 4
   ♠ A K 9 4                        ♠ Q 3 2
   ♡ Q 10 8 7 3          N          ♡ J 6
   ◊ 9 5 3           W       E       ◊ J 10 6 4 2
   ♣ 8                   S           ♣ 9 6 2
                    ♠ 8 7 5
                    ♡ A 5
                    ◊ A K Q 7
                    ♣ K Q 7 3
```

| West | North | East | South |
|------|-------|------|-------|
| *Delmouly* | *Tai* | *Bourchtoff* | *Huang* |
|  |  | Pass | 1♣ |
| 1♡ | 3♣ | Pass | 3♡ |
| Pass | 4♡ | Pass | 6♣ |
| All Pass |  |  |  |

---

At the other table Michel Lebel and Klotz had bid a sensible 3NT for France, picking up +630. What on earth happened here? Huang's 1♣ opening was Precision Club, promising 16 points or more. Tai's 3♣ was natural and game-forcing and two cue-bids in the enemy suit followed. Huang now wanted to be in a slam if his partner held a spade control but he had no bid to ask for this. (It seems to us that he should have signed off in 5♣, expecting partner to advance with a spade control.) He marked time by checking that the 1♡ overcall did indeed show a one-suiter, instead of some sort of two-suiter. "Yes, a one-suiter in hearts," came the reply. Huang now bid 6♣. Can you imagine how the contract was made?

Claude Delmouly led the ♠A and, in accordance with the signalling system being played, East's ♠2 showed an odd number of cards in the suit. Delmouly paused for thought. If East held only three spades, declarer would have leapt to 6♣ on a hand with no spade control, with a spade suit that was at best Q-x-x. Concluding that no-one could bid so badly at this level, Delmouly placed declarer with a singleton spade. In that case the only way to beat the contract was to find East with a void heart. He switched to a heart at Trick 2 and Huang had been reprieved from the gallows. He won with the ♡A and drew two rounds of trumps, West showing out on the second round. Huang now played his top diamonds, throwing two spades from dummy, and cross-ruffed his way to twelve tricks. That was a valuable +1370 and 12 IMPs for the Chinese team.

Do you blame Delmouly for his line of defence? Can you see any reason why he should have played another spade, instead of switching to hearts? If so, you are cleverer than we are! It seems to us that the Chinese South took a bold gamble in the bidding and part of the odds in favour of his leap to 6♣ was that the defenders might not – for one reason or another – take their available spade tricks.

We move next to the 1983 US trials. Again the contenders are all world-class players. Put yourself in the West hot seat and see if you would have done better than the great Jeff Meckstroth:

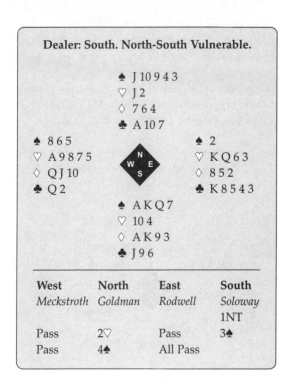

**Dealer: South. North-South Vulnerable.**

```
                    ♠ J 10 9 4 3
                    ♡ J 2
                    ◊ 7 6 4
                    ♣ A 10 7
♠ 8 6 5                           ♠ 2
♡ A 9 8 7 5           N           ♡ K Q 6 3
◊ Q J 10          W     E         ◊ 8 5 2
♣ Q 2                S            ♣ K 8 5 4 3
                    ♠ A K Q 7
                    ♡ 10 4
                    ◊ A K 9 3
                    ♣ J 9 6
```

| West | North | East | South |
|------|-------|------|-------|
| *Meckstroth* | *Goldman* | *Rodwell* | *Soloway* |
| | | | 1NT |
| Pass | 2♡ | Pass | 3♠ |
| Pass | 4♠ | All Pass | |

Paul Soloway broke the transfer and Bobbie Goldman boldly raised to the spade game. Meckstroth led an obvious ◊Q, drawing the ◊4, ◊2 and ◊3. What next?

It was unattractive to switch to hearts or clubs and Meckstroth did what most players would have done: he played another diamond. Soloway could now win, draw trumps and play two more diamond winners, discarding one of dummy's hearts. He subsequently played the club suit for one loser, conceding one trick in each side suit and making the game exactly.

To beat the game, Meckstroth needed to switch to hearts at Trick 2. Was there any way to find this switch? Most defenders give an attitude signal on a queen lead, in which case East's ◊2 would strongly imply that he did not hold a diamond honour. He might hold ◊A-K-2 and be fearful of overtaking in case West had led from ◊Q-x but such a lead was unlikely in the extreme. Nor was it plausible that East held ◊K-2, since he would play the king on the first round. It therefore seems that three small diamonds was a likely holding for East, albeit that it was unusual for declarer to duck in such circumstances.

Once West reads the diamond position, the danger of a heart being discarded from dummy on the long diamond is apparent. Also, South can be placed with most of his points in spades and diamonds, which increases the prospect of East holding the ♡K. So, reluctant as we mere mortals are to find fault with one of the world's greatest players, it seems that we cannot sign the same reprieve form that we awarded to Delmouly.

As we plunge deeper into the chapter, the hands get wilder. We next visit the 1993 Bermuda Bowl quarter-finals. USA-1 face the Netherlands and South has quite a bidding problem on this deal:

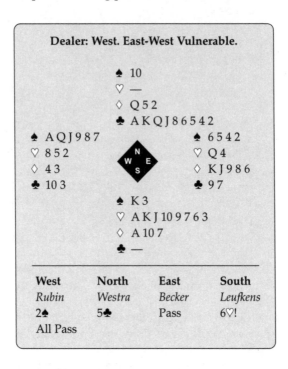

Dealer: West. East-West Vulnerable.

|  | ♠ 10 |  |
|  | ♡ — |  |
|  | ◇ Q 5 2 |  |
|  | ♣ A K Q J 8 6 5 4 2 |  |

| ♠ A Q J 9 8 7 |  | ♠ 6 5 4 2 |
| ♡ 8 5 2 |  | ♡ Q 4 |
| ◇ 4 3 |  | ◇ K J 9 8 6 |
| ♣ 10 3 |  | ♣ 9 7 |

|  | ♠ K 3 |  |
|  | ♡ A K J 10 9 7 6 3 |  |
|  | ◇ A 10 7 |  |
|  | ♣ — |  |

| West | North | East | South |
|------|-------|------|-------|
| *Rubin* | *Westra* | *Becker* | *Leufkens* |
| 2♠ | 5♣ | Pass | 6♡! |
| All Pass | | | |

Both Souths faced this bidding problem. The USA South decided to pass 5♣. An alternative was to raise to 6♣, which would have succeeded as the cards lie. What can one say of Leufkens' decision to jump to 6♡, with a void in partner's suit and so many losers in spades and diamonds? Well, let's be polite (for a change) and say that it cleverly protected the ♠K from the opening lead.

West led the ♠A, to look at the dummy. Suppose you had held the West cards. The dummy has been revealed, which was your intention when you chose the spade ace lead. What next?

Ron Rubin saw that there were two ways in which a club switch could gain. If East were void in clubs, a club ruff would dispatch the slam immediately. If instead East and South held one club each, a club switch might cut declarer off from the dummy. A club switch was likely to fail only in the unlikely situation that South had leapt to a slam with a void in his partner's suit. Admirable reasoning, no doubt, but the club switch proved so disastrous that it would one day merit a place in a chapter on 'Horrible Defences at Trick 2'. Leufkens was able to discard both his losing diamonds and when the queen of trumps fell doubleton he had his slam. "Well bid, partner!"

We have not yet addressed the question of how East should signal at Trick 1. When dummy holds a singleton in the suit led and can ruff a continuation in that suit, it is normal for East's signal to be suit preference. Here, however, dummy was void in trumps. East's signal should therefore be 'attitude' on an ace lead. (If West held the ♠A-K, he would lead the king, requesting a count signal.) So, East's signal of the ♠2 has no bearing on his holding in clubs. It merely denies the ♠K, unless he happens to hold ♠K-2. Our inclination is to award no blame on the deal and to leave it as 'just one of those things'.

It's always good to end a chapter with a bang and the next deal should prove no disappointment in that respect. It comes from a semi-final of the 1997 Vanderbilt in Dallas. Hold on to your seats!

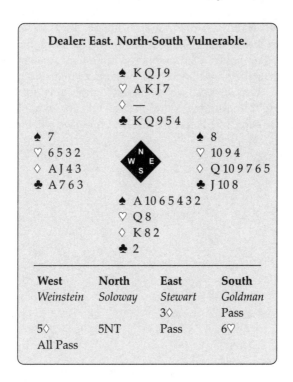

**Dealer: East. North-South Vulnerable.**

|  | ♠ K Q J 9 |  |
|---|---|---|
|  | ♡ A K J 7 |  |
|  | ◇ — |  |
|  | ♣ K Q 9 5 4 |  |
| ♠ 7 |  | ♠ 8 |
| ♡ 6 5 3 2 |  | ♡ 10 9 4 |
| ◇ A J 4 3 |  | ◇ Q 10 9 7 6 5 |
| ♣ A 7 6 3 |  | ♣ J 10 8 |
|  | ♠ A 10 6 5 4 3 2 |  |
|  | ♡ Q 8 |  |
|  | ◇ K 8 2 |  |
|  | ♣ 2 |  |

| West | North | East | South |
|---|---|---|---|
| Weinstein | Soloway | Stewart | Goldman |
|  |  | 3◇ | Pass |
| 5◇ | 5NT | Pass | 6♡ |
| All Pass |  |  |  |

Paul Soloway's 5NT was intended as a general 'pick a slam' request. Bobbie Goldman read it as the Unusual No-trump and consequently expected his partner to hold a big two-suiter in hearts and clubs. He gave preference to hearts and ended in a 4-2 fit when there was a 7-4 fit available in spades!

Steve Weinstein led the $\diamond$A and was no doubt surprised to hear declarer request a spade discard from dummy. Goldman was forced to discard, of course, because he could not afford to shorten dummy's trumps. If the defenders cashed a club trick next, so be it. It may seem obvious for West to play the ♣A next but from his point of view it was impossible for his club trick to run away. South held at most eight cards in the red suits, so dummy's spades could not provide sufficient club discards from the South hand. Nor, it seemed, could all five clubs be discarded from dummy. Meanwhile, if declarer was in a 4-3 fit, a second round of diamonds might cause him to lose control.

Famous last words! Declarer won the diamond continuation with the king, throwing a club from dummy, and drew trumps in four rounds. He then unleashed his spade suit, throwing four more clubs from the dummy. "Just the twelve, partner!"

How much blame shall we assess in a Westerly direction? Lenient as we tend to be . . . it would be too generous to allow West to escape free of charge. When dummy discarded on the ace lead, we would expect East to give a discouraging signal in diamonds, denying the king. There could then be no point in a diamond continuation. Against that, it was difficult in the extreme for Weinstein to visualize that all dummy's clubs might vanish. It had been a clever psychological move for Goldman to throw a spade from dummy, rather than a club. So, with a light censure to West (we're sure he will cash his ♣A next time) we will move on to the next chapter.

# 8
# Record-breaking Pre-empts

Go to your local second-hand book shop and ask the guy behind the counter if he has any bridge books. "I think we have a few upstairs, far left-hand corner on the top shelf." You climb the wooden stairs and eventually find yourself paging through some dusty bidding manual, written in 1942. The chapter on pre-empts will recommend that for an opening three-bid you should have six playing tricks when non-vulnerable and seven playing tricks when vulnerable. The typical suit quality required in those days was not far short of K-Q-J-x-x-x. Some authorities even recommended that you should have a 'side ace', so you could reach the winners if playing in no-trumps.

A modern three-level pre-emptive opening, when non-vulnerable at any rate, promises thirteen cards but not much more than that. Our first example of a weak pre-empt comes from the 2001 Vanderbilt and both East players opened 3♣ with a jack-high suit. This is commonplace nowadays but was no doubt worthy of a short prison sentence back in 1942. However, the two pre-emptors did not share the same fate.

---

**Dealer: East. North-South Vulnerable.**

|  | ♠ K 9 8 |  |
|---|---|---|
|  | ♡ J 10 9 4 3 |  |
|  | ◇ K 9 7 5 |  |
|  | ♣ Q |  |

| ♠ A Q 10 7 |  | ♠ J 4 2 |
|---|---|---|
| ♡ K Q 5 |  | ♡ 7 2 |
| ◇ 4 2 |  | ◇ J |
| ♣ A K 9 3 |  | ♣ J 10 7 6 5 4 2 |

|  | ♠ 6 5 3 |  |
|---|---|---|
|  | ♡ A 8 6 |  |
|  | ◇ A Q 10 8 6 3 |  |
|  | ♣ 8 |  |

| West | North | East | South |
|---|---|---|---|
| Petrunin | Rosenberg | Gromov | Zia |
|  |  | 3♣ | 3◇ |
| 4♣ | 5◇ | Pass | Pass |
| Dbl | All Pass |  |  |

---

Andrei Gromov's light pre-empt pushed Zia to a light overcall. Aleksander Petrunin raised softly to 4♣, as he might have done with 10 points fewer. Concluding that Zia had a strong hand, Michael Rosenberg jumped to the diamond game. After two passes a Siberian tiger emerged from the bushes. Double!

Petrunin led a high club and then cunningly switched to the ♠Q. Zia was not fooled: he went up with the king, drew trumps and exited in spades. East could win the second round of spades with the jack and play one heart through declarer's ace. However, when West won with the ♡Q he had no good return. East had no second entry in the spade suit, so after cashing a spade West had to return a heart into declarer's split tenace (or concede a ruff-and-discard.) That was still 500 for the Russians. What do you think would happen at the other table? This was the bidding:

| West | North | East | South |
|------|-------|------|-------|
| *Cohen* | *Balicki* | *Berkowitz* | *Zmudzinski* |
| | | 3♣ | Pass |
| 3NT | All Pass | | |

Perhaps because of South's silence, Larry Cohen was much more ambitious than his counterpart. A club game seemed a long way off (he had no reason to imagine a singleton diamond opposite), so he tried his luck in 3NT. Once in a while East would provide a diamond stopper. If he didn't, perhaps North would lead a major suit and nine tricks could be run before the defenders found their diamond tricks.

One of Cohen's wishes was granted when Cezary Balicki led a heart. Unfortunately Adam Zmudzinski won his partner's ♡J lead with the ace and switched to a deadly ◊Q. (It was a good hand for the 'Strong Ten' method of opening leads where the lead of a jack denies any higher honour.) The Poles soon had seven tricks before them and added 150 to the 500 that their Russian team-mates had picked up. That was 12 IMPs for the Gromov squad, who went on to win the trophy.

Realising that a pre-empt on seven cards to the jack will impress few readers nowadays (and may even trigger a few letters of complaint), we will lower our sights to a suit of six cards to the ten. The deal arose in the 1992 Cap Gemini tournament and the perpetrator was England's Andrew Robson:

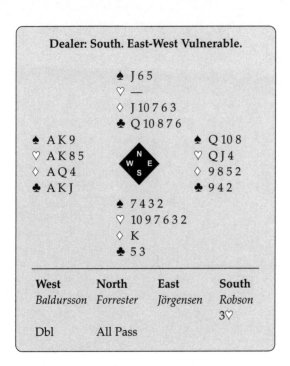

**Dealer: South. East-West Vulnerable.**

|  | ♠ J 6 5 |  |
|---|---|---|
|  | ♡ — |  |
|  | ◊ J 10 7 6 3 |  |
|  | ♣ Q 10 8 7 6 |  |
| ♠ A K 9 |  | ♠ Q 10 8 |
| ♡ A K 8 5 |  | ♡ Q J 4 |
| ◊ A Q 4 |  | ◊ 9 8 5 2 |
| ♣ A K J |  | ♣ 9 4 2 |
|  | ♠ 7 4 3 2 |  |
|  | ♡ 10 9 7 6 3 2 |  |
|  | ◊ K |  |
|  | ♣ 5 3 |  |

| West | North | East | South |
|---|---|---|---|
| Baldursson | Forrester | Jörgensen | Robson |
|  |  |  | 3♡ |
| Dbl | All Pass |  |  |

Playing against two Icelandic internationals, Andrew Robson opened with a pre-emptive 3♡ on his ten-high suit. Perhaps he was unaware that East-West had a penalty double in their armoury! Robson managed to take three tricks but the non-vulnerable penalty still amounted to 1400.

In a head-to-head match, you might hope for a 1-IMP gain if your team-mates achieved the dual feat of bidding 6NT and making 6NT. The Cap Gemini tournament calculates an IMP-swing against an average score (known as a 'datum') from the other tables. At four out of eight tables 6NT was reached. In every case North chose to lead the ◊J and declarer was able to score three diamond tricks for his contract. So, Robson's valiant/foolish/courageous (choose your adjective) pre-empt cost him 9 IMPs. Note that on a spade lead, which does not give away a trick, 6NT can be made by stripping North to ◊J ♣Q-10 and throwing him in with a diamond.

Extreme pre-empts are not exclusively a modern phenomenon and the next deal was played in the late 1960s. Henri Svarc, like most French champions, does not have a general penchant for undisciplined bidding. Perhaps he was in a mischievous mood when this deal arose:

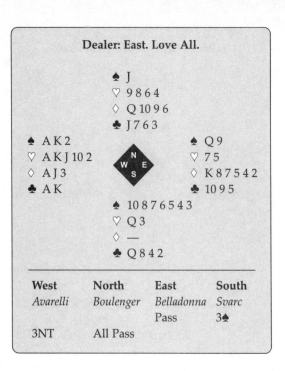

**Dealer: East. Love All.**

|  | ♠ J |  |
|---|---|---|
|  | ♡ 9 8 6 4 |  |
|  | ◇ Q 10 9 6 |  |
|  | ♣ J 7 6 3 |  |
| ♠ A K 2 |  | ♠ Q 9 |
| ♡ A K J 10 2 |  | ♡ 7 5 |
| ◇ A J 3 |  | ◇ K 8 7 5 4 2 |
| ♣ A K |  | ♣ 10 9 5 |
|  | ♠ 10 8 7 6 5 4 3 |  |
|  | ♡ Q 3 |  |
|  | ◇ — |  |
|  | ♣ Q 8 4 2 |  |

| West | North | East | South |
|---|---|---|---|
| *Avarelli* | *Boulenger* | *Belladonna* | *Svarc* |
|  |  | Pass | 3♠ |
| 3NT | All Pass |  |  |

Walter Avarelli had a take-out double available but he opted for the very conservative bid of 3NT. This became the final contract and the ♠J was led. Diamonds broke badly but this was offset by the fall of the ♡Q in two rounds. Declarer duly made twelve tricks and it seemed that Henri Svarc's atypical pre-empt (made at equal vulnerability in the second seat) might have drawn blood. A likely gain for the French, would you say?

Not exactly! This was the French pair's auction.

| West | North | East | South |
|---|---|---|---|
| *Tintner* | *Forquet* | *Stetten* | *Garozzo* |
|  |  | Pass | Pass |
| 2♣ | Pass | 2◇ | Pass |
| 2♡ | Pass | 3◇ | Pass |
| 5NT | Pass | 7◇ | All Pass |

At the other table, without any interference, East-West found their diamond fit. Léon Tintner's 5NT was the grand slam force and Stetten jumped to the grand, judging that his extra diamond length would compensate for the missing queen. Not today, because West held only three-card diamond support and the queen did not fall in two rounds.

The cruel trump break scuttled the grand, which went two down after a spade lead. Even a small slam in diamonds would have been doomed. So, Svarc's bold pre-empt resulted (yet again) in a big loss for his side. He prevented the opponents from reaching the apparently optimal contract on their cards. However, the unusual distribution in his hand was matched by a similarly distorted distribution in his partner's hand – enough to defeat an enemy slam.

On the deal we have just seen, the pre-empt prevented the opponents from reaching a losing slam. In our next exhibit, we'll see the other side of the coin: a pre-empt that pushes the opponents into a slam that is allowed to make.

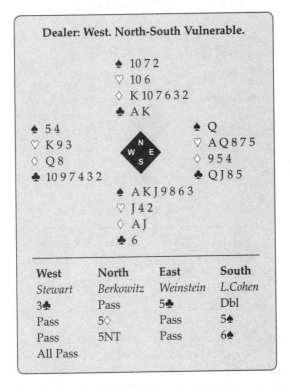

Dealer: West. North-South Vulnerable.

|  | ♠ 10 7 2 |  |
|  | ♡ 10 6 |  |
|  | ◊ K 10 7 6 3 2 |  |
|  | ♣ A K |  |

| ♠ 5 4 | | ♠ Q |
| ♡ K 9 3 | | ♡ A Q 8 7 5 |
| ◊ Q 8 | | ◊ 9 5 4 |
| ♣ 10 9 7 4 3 2 | | ♣ Q J 8 5 |

|  | ♠ A K J 9 8 6 3 |  |
|  | ♡ J 4 2 |  |
|  | ◊ A J |  |
|  | ♣ 6 |  |

| West | North | East | South |
| --- | --- | --- | --- |
| *Stewart* | *Berkowitz* | *Weinstein* | *L.Cohen* |
| 3♣ | Pass | 5♣ | Dbl |
| Pass | 5◊ | Pass | 5♠ |
| Pass | 5NT | Pass | 6♠ |
| All Pass | | | |

The deal comes from the Round of 16 in the 1997 Spingold. As you see, Fred Stewart's pre-empt pushed the opponents to a slam with two top losers. South's bidding had suggested powerful values, however, and a heart lead into that hand was far from obvious. Stewart eventually led a club and declarer could now win, draw trumps and set up the diamond suit. All thirteen tricks were made.

At the other table West passed and Ralph Katz opened a weak (not so weak, really) 2◊ on the North cards. As a result his partner, Richard

Pavlicek, played in the normal 4♠ contract. Ironically, in this room, where it didn't really matter, Jeff Wolfson found the heart lead and held declarer to eleven tricks.

Since all our previous examples shed a negative light on particularly weak pre-empts, let's balance them with a counter-example that arose at the *Politiken* Invitational of 1997. It shows another kind of atypical pre-emptive opening: one made in the third or fourth seat with an abnormally strong hand. Rarely used by lesser mortals, it is fairly common practice among experts.

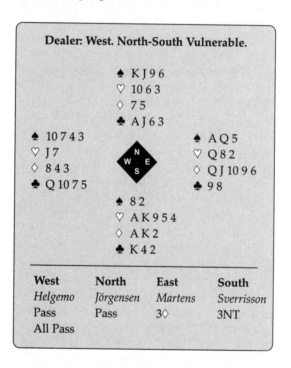

**Dealer: West. North-South Vulnerable.**

|  | ♠ K J 9 6 |  |
|  | ♡ 10 6 3 |  |
|  | ◊ 7 5 |  |
|  | ♣ A J 6 3 |  |
| ♠ 10 7 4 3 |  | ♠ A Q 5 |
| ♡ J 7 |  | ♡ Q 8 2 |
| ◊ 8 4 3 |  | ◊ Q J 10 9 6 |
| ♣ Q 10 7 5 |  | ♣ 9 8 |
|  | ♠ 8 2 |  |
|  | ♡ A K 9 5 4 |  |
|  | ◊ A K 2 |  |
|  | ♣ K 4 2 |  |

| West | North | East | South |
|------|-------|------|-------|
| Helgemo | Jörgensen | Martens | Sverrisson |
| Pass | Pass | 3◊ | 3NT |
| All Pass | | | |

Declarer won the first round of diamonds and played ace, king and another heart. The suit broke 3-2 and it was the pre-empter who won the third round, West throwing a spade. Declarer ducked the next round of diamonds and won the diamond continuation, raising an eyebrow when West followed on the third round. Declarer cashed the two long hearts, West throwing two more spades and East one spade and one diamond winner.

At this stage declarer had eight top tricks: four hearts and two ace-kings in the minors. What was the best chance of a ninth trick? It seemed entirely possible that East (who had not thrown a club) was retaining a guard on the ♣Q. It was also possible that West held the ♠A. Indeed, the only other possibility was that East had indulged in a five-card pre-empt when holding at least 9 points in a balanced hand. His mind made up, Sigurdur Sverrisson led a spade to the king. East won and cashed the one diamond winner that he had retained. The ♠Q was the setting trick. "Did you have the queen of clubs, too?" asked Sverrisson in a resigned tone. "No, I have it here," said West.

At nearly every other table, East opened at the one level and North-South easily made game in hearts or no-trumps. Geir Helgemo and Krysztof Martens picked up a 12-IMP swing against the datum score.

We are approaching the end of our brief fly-past of the world of pre-empts and we're aware that you may have been somewhat underwhelmed by the fare on offer so far ("At our club we regularly open vulnerable pre-empts on Q-x-x-x-x!"). We accept the charge, although no refunds will be offered on the book as a whole. In our defence we'd like to say that where anything goes nothing is really exceptional. We will round off the chapter with one of our stronger offerings, played in a New Zealand trials and originally reported by Omar Sharif in one of his columns.

The deal arose in the New Zealand trials for the 1996 Rhodes Olympiad. You may want to consider it as a play problem. How would you play a grand slam in clubs when West leads the ♡J?

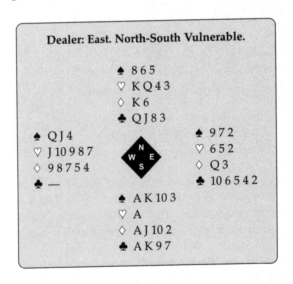

**Dealer: East. North-South Vulnerable.**

```
                    ♠ 8 6 5
                    ♡ K Q 4 3
                    ◇ K 6
                    ♣ Q J 8 3
    ♠ Q J 4                         ♠ 9 7 2
    ♡ J 10 9 8 7        N           ♡ 6 5 2
    ◇ 9 8 7 5 4     W       E       ◇ Q 3
    ♣ —                S            ♣ 10 6 5 4 2
                    ♠ A K 10 3
                    ♡ A
                    ◇ A J 10 2
                    ♣ A K 9 7
```

Michael Ware won the heart lead with the bare ace and paused to assess his prospects. The two spade losers could be thrown on the ♡K and ♡Q. He therefore needed to make arrangements only for the two diamond losers. When declarer played a diamond to the king and a second round of diamonds, the queen appeared from East. Brilliant! All that remained to do was to draw trumps and claim the grand slam bonus.

This pleasant prospect had to be put on hold when declarer played the ace of trumps and West showed out, discarding a diamond. To make the grand now, declarer needed to score his seven side-suit winners, the one round of trumps already drawn and five of the remaining six trumps on a cross-ruff. Embarking on this line, declarer ruffed the good ◊J high in the dummy. Unfortunately East threw a heart and declarer could no longer score the three heart tricks that he needed. When he attempted to cash two more hearts, East ruffed the third round. Although declarer could overruff, he was saddled with an unavoidable spade loser.

Do you see how the grand slam might have been made? Ware was not too far away from the winning line, which is to cash the ♣A at Trick 2, discovering the 5-0 break. Cash your two top spades and play the two diamond winners, ending in the dummy. East has not yet had the opportunity to discard a heart, so you can cash the ♡K and ♡Q, throwing your two spade losers. These cards remain:

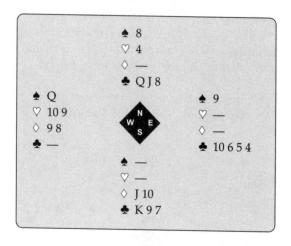

The rest is easy. You ruff the ♠8 in the South hand and ruff a diamond high. You then ruff the ♡4 in the South hand and ruff your last diamond high. The trump king will take the final trick and East will have had the dubious pleasure of underruffing you three times. Life was not meant to be fun!

An interesting play hand, certainly, but no doubt you are wondering what on earth it is doing in a chapter on dodgy pre-empts. The answer is that at the other table East, David Ackerley, opened 3♣! He was buoyed both by the vulnerability and the fact that his team was trailing by some margin. North-South brushed aside the pre-empt to reach and easily make 6NT, which translated to a 14-IMP gain. You may think that there is an element of justice to this. But, frankly, had you ever heard of someone pre-empting in a suit in which the opponents could make a grand slam?

*Bridge Hands to Make You Laugh . . . and Cry*

# 9
# Who Needs a 7-5 Fit?

The deal below arose during a match in the 1999 *Forbo* tournament. Consider it first as a bidding problem from South's point of view:

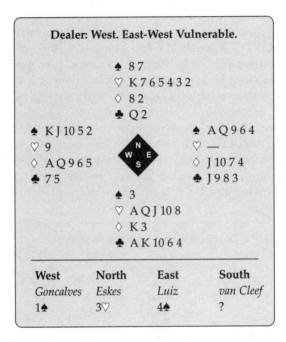

**Dealer: West. East-West Vulnerable.**

```
                    ♠ 87
                    ♡ K 7 6 5 4 3 2
                    ◇ 82
                    ♣ Q 2
    ♠ K J 10 5 2              ♠ A Q 9 6 4
    ♡ 9              N         ♡ —
    ◇ A Q 9 6 5   W   E       ◇ J 10 7 4
    ♣ 7 5             S        ♣ J 9 8 3
                    ♠ 3
                    ♡ A Q J 10 8
                    ◇ K 3
                    ♣ A K 10 6 4
```

| West | North | East | South |
|------|-------|------|-------|
| *Goncalves* | *Eskes* | *Luiz* | *van Cleef* |
| 1♠ | 3♡ | 4♠ | ? |

What would you bid? It would be easy to bid a two-way 5♡ – perhaps a make, perhaps a good sacrifice. Van Cleef found the 'expert's bid' of 5♣. This was intended as a fit-non-jump. In other words, it showed a raise to 5♡ but was also lead-directing, should East-West advance in spades. The situation was unclear to North and the 5♣ bid was passed out. How would you play this contract when West leads the ♣5?

If you run the lead to your ♣10, the suit will be blocked. You could play the ♣A next, dropping dummy's queen and hoping for a 3-3 break. Alternatively, you could cross to the ♣Q and lead a spade, setting up a ruffing entry to your hand. You would then be at the mercy of a defensive heart ruff or a diamond switch from East through your king.

Jan van Cleef judged that West would not have led from the ♣J. He rose with dummy's ♣Q at Trick 1 and finessed the ♣10 successfully. He could then draw the remaining trumps and run seven rounds of hearts.

"I should have led my singleton heart, looking for a ruff!" said West.

# 10
# The Heavenly Opening Lead

ook at any table of 'Recommended Opening Leads' and you will find the undisputed champion perched at the top: A-K-x-x. When you are on lead against a suit contract and you hold a side suit headed by the ace-king, you need a very good reason indeed to look elsewhere. Edgar Kaplan, a great player and for many years the publisher of USA's *Bridge World*, had powerful feelings on the matter. "When God gives you an ace-king combination," said Kaplan, "He is telling you what to lead." Kaplan once wrote, tongue-in-cheek, that a swing arose when a certain player *impiously* did not lead his God-given sequence.

Rules are meant to be broken, of course, and there are many occasions on which the 'safe' lead of an ace-king turns out to be very unsafe indeed. Let's see an example featuring the great Roger Trézel, one of the very few players to have won the fabled Triple Crown (world championships in Pairs, Open Teams and Olympiad).

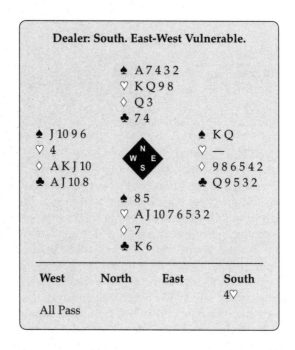

```
Dealer: South. East-West Vulnerable.

                    ♠ A 7 4 3 2
                    ♡ K Q 9 8
                    ◇ Q 3
                    ♣ 7 4
    ♠ J 10 9 6              ♠ K Q
    ♡ 4            N        ♡ —
    ◇ A K J 10   W   E      ◇ 9 8 6 5 4 2
    ♣ A J 10 8     S        ♣ Q 9 5 3 2
                    ♠ 8 5
                    ♡ A J 10 7 6 5 3 2
                    ◇ 7
                    ♣ K 6
```

| West | North | East | South |
|------|-------|------|-------|
|      |       |      | 4♡    |
| All Pass |   |      |       |

Trézel opened 4♡ and West did not seem to realise that some action was called for on his hand. A double was the obvious move and would surely be the unanimous choice of any bidding panel nowadays. When it came to the opening lead, however, West was quick to spot his God-given sequence. He led the ◇A, followed by the king. Suppose you had been South. How would you have played?

On the second round of diamonds Trézel cleverly discarded a spade instead of ruffing. West switched to a trump but declarer ruffed the spades good for a club discard and made his game. Do you see the point of the spade discard? It made it possible to set up the spades without allowing East, the 'danger hand', to gain the lead.

What would have happened if West had switched to a spade at Trick 2? It's not good enough because declarer can win and play the ◇Q himself, throwing a spade. Once again he will be able to set up the spades without allowing East on lead. Only a spade lead beats 4♡. Was there a small hint from Up Above? West had at least been given J-10-9-x in the suit! When the play was over, West escaped any criticism for his choice of opening lead. East was too busy explaining that a small slam was cold their way in either minor and that West must have been "asleep, do you hear me, partner?" not to have doubled on his hand.

In what situations might you ignore an ace-king and make some different lead? When the opponents have sacrificed at a high level on scarce values, a trump lead is often effective. That's because their only chance of picking up a respectable number of tricks will be to score ruffs in the short-trump hand.

Some defenders like to lead from the ace-king anyway, to look at the dummy. It can then be too late for a trump lead. An example of this arose in the Hammamet World Championship of 1997, when Brazil faced France:

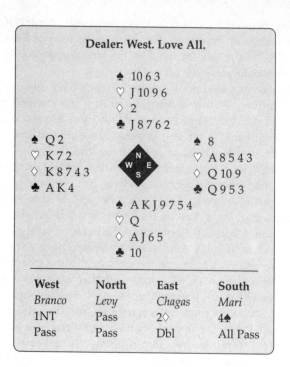

**Dealer: West. Love All.**

```
                    ♠ 10 6 3
                    ♡ J 10 9 6
                    ◇ 2
                    ♣ J 8 7 6 2
  ♠ Q 2                              ♠ 8
  ♡ K 7 2              N             ♡ A 8 5 4 3
  ◇ K 8 7 4 3     W        E        ◇ Q 10 9
  ♣ A K 4              S             ♣ Q 9 5 3
                    ♠ A K J 9 7 5 4
                    ♡ Q
                    ◇ A J 6 5
                    ♣ 10
```

| West | North | East | South |
|------|-------|------|-------|
| *Branco* | *Levy* | *Chagas* | *Mari* |
| 1NT | Pass | 2◇ | 4♠ |
| Pass | Pass | Dbl | All Pass |

With a respectful glance upwards, Marcelo Branco led the ♣A. Dummy, with its ruffing value in diamonds was not a pleasant sight. Branco switched hastily to a trump but it was too late. Do you see how the club lead had helped declarer? It had set up a quick route to his hand, which would enable him to take two diamond ruffs. Christian Mari won the trump switch, cashed the ◇A and ruffed a diamond. He was then able to return to his hand with a club ruff and ruff a second diamond. Game made!

It was not attractive to lead a trump from Q-x. When a trump lead is called for, however, you should be willing to lead from an unattractive holding. Here Branco had little reason to expect a ruffing value in the dummy and it would have been a brilliant shot to lead a trump. (It has to be the ♠2 rather than the ♠Q or declarer has the entries to concede two hearts and establish two tricks in the suit for diamond discards.)

In our next example, from the 1992 Spingold, the great Dealer had been unusually generous. The expert on lead against a high-level contract had not one but two ace-king combinations in his hand:

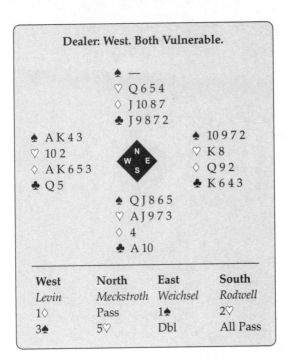

**Dealer: West. Both Vulnerable.**

```
              ♠ —
              ♡ Q 6 5 4
              ◇ J 10 8 7
              ♣ J 9 8 7 2
♠ A K 4 3                      ♠ 10 9 7 2
♡ 10 2          N             ♡ K 8
◇ A K 6 5 3   W   E           ◇ Q 9 2
♣ Q 5           S             ♣ K 6 4 3
              ♠ Q J 8 6 5
              ♡ A J 9 7 3
              ◇ 4
              ♣ A 10
```

| West | North | East | South |
|------|-------|------|-------|
| *Levin* | *Meckstroth* | *Weichsel* | *Rodwell* |
| 1◇ | Pass | 1♠ | 2♡ |
| 3♠ | 5♡ | Dbl | All Pass |

Eric Rodwell's vulnerable 2♡ overcall would certainly not be found in any text-book, particularly as he had such a powerful spade holding. He cannot have enjoyed the sight of his partner making an advance sacrifice over 3♠! (At the other table 4♠ went two down doubled.) Suppose you had been West. What would you have led?

Bobby Levin led the ♠A, ruffed in the dummy, and Rodwell found the key play – a diamond, to open a ruffing route to his hand. The contract then rolled home with the aid of a ruffing finesse in spades, a further spade ruff and an eventual trump finesse. A trump lead would have sealed declarer's fate. West would also survive a lead from the other ace-king, in diamonds, provided he played a heart or a diamond at Trick 2.

Should West have led a trump? It's easy for us to look at the diagram and say: "Fairly obvious against such a high-level sacrifice". It was quite possible, though, that North-South held the hearts and the clubs, and would score sufficient tricks unless East-West could cash three winners in the other suits first. What can we conclude from this? Well, we knew it already, but there is a fair amount of luck in the game of bridge. Indeed, it is one of its greatest assets that the luck and skill are so perfectly balanced.

So far the lead from ace-king was not the killing one. Sometimes the situation is worse and a lead from ace-king is the only one to give away the contract. Here is an example from Pakistan *vs* USA in the 1984 World Team Olympiad:

**Dealer: East. Love All.**

```
                    ♠ Q J 7 3
                    ♡ A 10 7 6 5
                    ◊ A 4 2
                    ♣ 2
  ♠ A 10 8 4 2                      ♠ K 6
  ♡ 9 3             N              ♡ 8 2
  ◊ 5 3          W     E           ◊ K Q 10 9 8 7
  ♣ A K 9 7         S              ♣ 8 5 4
                    ♠ 9 5
                    ♡ K Q J 4
                    ◊ J 6
                    ♣ Q J 10 6 3
```

| West | North | East | South |
|------|-------|------|-------|
| Soloway | Nisar | Goldman | Nishat |
| | | 3◊ | Pass |
| Pass | Dbl | Pass | 4♡ |
| Dbl | All Pass | | |

Paul Soloway, of the USA, doubled 4♡ and led the ♣K. It was easy now for Abedi Nishat, of Pakistan, to establish the clubs for several discards. Away went the diamond losers in dummy and he registered +590. If West leads any other suit, the defence must prevail. On a trump lead, for example, declarer can win and lead a club, eventually setting up two club winners. He can reach them only with a fourth round of trumps and that will prevent him from discarding dummy's diamonds and taking a diamond ruff.

In the other room the auction was different, making North (Bob Hamman) declarer in 4♡ doubled. It was obvious for Saleem Masood to lead the ◊K and that exposed four losers from which declarer had no escape.

Let's end the chapter with a deal where a defender managed to resist the temptation of leading from an ace-king more than once. You may know the deal but it is worth repeating. It arose in the 1975 Bermuda Bowl round robin, with Italy facing USA:

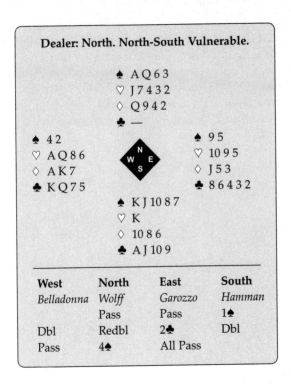

**Dealer: North. North-South Vulnerable.**

```
                    ♠ A Q 6 3
                    ♡ J 7 4 3 2
                    ◇ Q 9 4 2
                    ♣ —
    ♠ 4 2                           ♠ 9 5
    ♡ A Q 8 6                       ♡ 10 9 5
    ◇ A K 7                         ◇ J 5 3
    ♣ K Q 7 5                       ♣ 8 6 4 3 2
                    ♠ K J 10 8 7
                    ♡ K
                    ◇ 10 8 6
                    ♣ A J 10 9
```

| West | North | East | South |
|------|-------|------|-------|
| *Belladonna* | *Wolff* | *Garozzo* | *Hamman* |
| | Pass | Pass | 1♠ |
| Dbl | Redbl | 2♣ | Dbl |
| Pass | 4♠ | All Pass | |

The lead of a top diamond would have left declarer with no problems. He would lose just two diamonds and a heart. Perhaps you think that this is all declarer should lose anyway. Let's see what happened after Giorgio Belladonna, whose hand was bristling with good cards in the side suits, decided to lead a trump.

Bob Hamman won in hand and played the ♡K. Belladonna won with the ace and switched to . . . the ◇7! Hamman now had to divine whether West's diamonds included the jack, in which case he should run the diamond to his hand, or whether Belladonna held the ◇A-K and had spurned a lead of the suit. Who can blame him for playing low from dummy, subsequently suffering the loss of three diamond tricks?

At the other table, against 4♠ doubled, Billy Eisenberg also found the excellent trump lead. However, the Italian South, Pittala, won and immediately played a diamond from hand. Eisenberg took his ace-king and persisted with a third round. Vito Pittala eventually discarded his heart on the thirteenth diamond, ruffed out West's club honours and recorded 990 for a doubled overtrick and 14 IMPs to Italy.

What do you conclude from these deals? That the ace-king lead should be moved from the top of the Recommended Leads table to the bottom? Of course not. For every deal where such a lead misfires there will be ten or twenty where it would have worked very well. If, some time in the future, you are on lead and decide to turn a blind eye to an ace-king combination in your hand . . . don't blame us if it goes wrong.

There is, however, a special situation where it may be ill advised to lead an ace-king. This is when you hold the God-given sequence but your partner has called for some different lead during the auction. In that case, ignore the suggestion from above and obey your partner. God always forgives, as we all know, but partners very seldom do!

# 11
# Short Measure

"An overcall at the one level requires a five-card suit. At the two level you should have a six-card suit." Good advice for beginners, yes, but experts are willing to take risks in order to disrupt the enemy auction. They make plenty of overcalls that would be deemed unsound by any reputable bridge teacher.

Overcalls on a four-card suit are almost always perpetrated at the one level, of course. Only in exceptional cases have there been higher-level overcalls on a four-carder. One prominent example comes from the 1985 Vanderbilt semi-final, a hard-fought match in which the Rodwell team was leading by 9 IMPs when this board, the very last of the match, hit the table:

**Dealer: South. North-South Vulnerable.**

```
              ♠ A J 8 7
              ♡ A Q 9
              ◇ 10 7 4
              ♣ A K 7
♠ 5 3 2                      ♠ K 10 9 6
♡ 10 7          N            ♡ 3 2
◇ Q 3 2      W     E         ◇ J 9 8 6 5
♣ J 9 6 5 2     S            ♣ Q 3
              ♠ Q 4
              ♡ K J 8 6 5 4
              ◇ A K
              ♣ 10 8 4
```

| West | North | East | South |
|------|-------|------|-------|
| Rosenberg | Rubin | Katz | Becker |
|  |  |  | 1♡ |
| Pass | 2♣* | 2♠! | Pass |
| Pass | 3NT | All Pass |  |
| *Artificial game-forcing relay. | | | |

In the Closed Room, Ralph Katz "risked an emaciated overcall rather than listen to eleven rounds of relay bidding", according to the report in *Bridge World*. As it was, North-South scored twelve easy tricks (conceding one to the ♠K) and picked up a disappointing 690.

North-South in the Open Room now had a chance to win the match by bidding and making the slam at the other table. However, it seems that bidding on ♠K-10-9-6 had a strange, almost irresistible appeal:

| West | North | East | South |
|------|-------|------|-------|
| *Meckstroth* | *Bramley* | *Rodwell* | *Bluhm* |
| | | | 1♡ |
| Pass | 2NT* | 3♠! | 4♡ |
| All Pass | | | |

*Jacoby, game-forcing heart raise.

Bart Bramley showed a forcing raise with the Jacoby 2NT bid and Eric Rodwell found the courage to bid his four-carder one level higher than Katz! What do you make of Bluhm's 4♡ bid now? Most partnerships would surely play this as the weakest move available. You are, after all, cutting out partner's chance of making a cue-bid at the four level. Bramley clearly interpreted 4♡ in this light, since he made no further move on his hand despite holding five great cards including the ace of the enemy suit. The match was therefore lost. If South could not bid 4◇ (because it would indicate a two-suiter in their variation of Jacoby), it does seem that he should have passed at his second turn. His hand was not unsuitable for slam purposes, with a six-card trump suit and a valuable ace-king outside. Over 4♣ from partner he could have continued with 4◇, surely enough to push North onto the slam path.

Look back to Rodwell's overcall. Although neither of the present authors would have considered it, some might say that 3♠ isn't that courageous. After all, the vulnerable opponents have a known major-suit fit so it is highly improbable that they will choose to stop and punish 3♠.

There is some truth in this, perhaps, so what about a four-level overcall on a four-carder? Unlike lower-level spade overcalls, overcalling 4♠ usually has an aura of finality about it. You accept that you will probably play there and are likely to be doubled. So, overcalling 4♠ on a four-card suit is certainly courageous. Nonetheless, there are several examples in our archives. Here is the most recent exhibit, which occurred in the 2003 Dutch Open teams final:

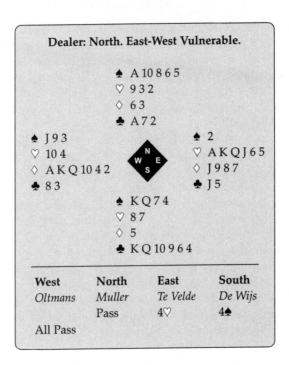

Dealer: North. East-West Vulnerable.

```
              ♠ A 10 8 6 5
              ♡ 9 3 2
              ◇ 6 3
              ♣ A 7 2
♠ J 9 3                          ♠ 2
♡ 10 4                           ♡ A K Q J 6 5
◇ A K Q 10 4 2      N            ◇ J 9 8 7
♣ 8 3           W     E          ♣ J 5
                    S
              ♠ K Q 7 4
              ♡ 8 7
              ◇ 5
              ♣ K Q 10 9 6 4
```

| West | North | East | South |
|------|-------|------|-------|
| Oltmans | Muller | Te Velde | De Wijs |
| | Pass | 4♡ | 4♠ |
| All Pass | | | |

Edgar Kaplan once famously remarked that the main drawback of a 4♡ opening bid is that it frequently functions as a left-handed transfer – it sort of compels LHO to bid 4♠. This was proved true here, when Bert Te Velde opted for a 4♡ opening opposite an unpassed partner. What do you make of this bid, by the way? We quite admire it, since the hand satisfies the main criterion for pre-emptive action: you will make considerably more tricks if you choose trumps than if you defend.

If the motive behind the 4♡ opening was to deter a spade bid from the opponents, it misfired dramatically. Indeed, it prompted Simon de Wijs to overcall 4♠ on his short and not particularly chunky suit! If the North and West hands had been switched, de Wijs might not have had such fond memories of the deal. As it was, he hit the jackpot, buying an extremely suitable dummy. When West led the ◇A and ◇K, declarer made twelve tricks.

How should the defence go? If you play 'ace for attitude, king for count' leads, West should lead the ◇K to ask for a count signal. To assist partner to distinguish between two and four cards, partner should signal with his second highest card from four. Here East will play the ◇9 and declarer will follow with the ◇5. Looking at the diamond suit in isolation it is still slightly more likely that East has the doubleton diamond, despite his ◇9 fitting into the scheme of second-best from J-9-8-7. However, if East does hold only two diamonds, it is almost impossible that he can overruff the dummy's ♠10 when a third round of diamonds is played. On that basis West should switch to the ♡10 at Trick 2. Three rounds of hearts will then put declarer to a guess for the contract. To succeed he will have to ruff the third heart with the king, cash the trump queen and finesse the ♠10. No doubt partner would be surprised to see a finesse in the trump suit, when putting down A-10-x-x-x in support of a four-level overcall!

At the other table, East opened a more orthodox 1♡. The bidding continued 2♣, 2◇, 2♠ around the table and the two-way double fit came to light. East-West found the profitable 5◇ sacrifice and went only one down to gain 9 IMPs for their side.

Having exhausted the topic of four-card overcalls, let's move to fresh pastures. What about overcalls on a three-card suit? There have been some examples, especially from the days of old when bidding was more free-wheeling. In the majority of the cases, these were semi-psychic 1♠ overcalls at favourable vulnerability – purely disruptive efforts. Neatly avoiding the risk that you may find such bids unimpressive, we will show you a three-card overcall at the two level, one that was eminently constructive. It comes from a 1950 international match between Great Britain and Norway, played in Brighton:

```
                    Dealer: West. Love All.

                    ♠ 10 8 7 4 3 2
                    ♡ 8 6 4
                    ◇ 10 5
                    ♣ K 2
    ♠ 9 5                            ♠ K 6
    ♡ Q 3 2              N           ♡ A 10 9 7
    ◇ A J 9         W       E        ◇ Q 8 7 3
    ♣ A J 9 8 4         S            ♣ 10 7 3
                    ♠ A Q J
                    ♡ K J 5
                    ◇ K 6 4 2
                    ♣ Q 6 5
```

| West | North | East | South |
|------|-------|------|-------|
|      | *Dodds* |    | *Konstam* |
| 1♣   | Pass  | 1♡   | Pass |
| 2♡   | Pass  | Pass | 2♠! |
| Pass | Pass  | 2NT  | Pass |
| Pass | 3♠    | All Pass |  |

Kenneth Konstam didn't feel like overcalling 1NT at his first round (far too mundane), so he passed. When the 2♡ bid came back to him, he produced a remarkable 2♠ overcall on his three-carder, correctly deducing that his partner must have some spade length. As it turned out, Leslie Dodds had rather better than average support!

Against the eventual contract of 3♠, West led the ♡2 to East's ace. Back came a diamond, ducked to West's jack. After a trump to king and ace, Konstam played a club to the king and drew the outstanding trump. The ♣Q compelled West to win. He exited safely (or so it seemed) with the ♣J but Konstam cleverly discarded a diamond from dummy. West was end-played! A club would give a ruff-and-discard (dummy throwing a heart loser); a diamond would set up a trick for the king and a heart would run into South's king-jack tenace. Nine tricks made, after one of the most inventive overcalls on record.

What about overcalls on a doubleton? There have been constructed specimens in an article parodying Mike Lawrence's penchant for overcalls on a four-card suit, but so far we haven't found any examples from real-life play. Moreover, any such effort would be classified as an outright psychic, rather than a tactical, bid, so we need not take it into account.

Since we are approaching the end of our journey through the world of overcalls, it may be fitting to end with some fireworks. We will show you a deal bristling with psychic pyrotechnics in both bidding and the play. It arose in the rarefied atmosphere of a world championship in a 1953 Bermuda Bowl match between Sweden and USA. It is a very famous deal and rightly so:

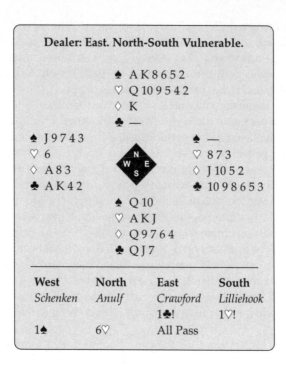

**Dealer: East. North-South Vulnerable.**

```
                    ♠ A K 8 6 5 2
                    ♡ Q 10 9 5 4 2
                    ◊ K
                    ♣ —
♠ J 9 7 4 3                         ♠ —
♡ 6                                 ♡ 8 7 3
◊ A 8 3                             ◊ J 10 5 2
♣ A K 4 2                           ♣ 10 9 8 6 5 3
                    ♠ Q 10
                    ♡ A K J
                    ◊ Q 9 7 6 4
                    ♣ Q J 7
```

| West | North | East | South |
|------|-------|------|-------|
| *Schenken* | *Anulf* | *Crawford* | *Lilliehook* |
| | | 1♣! | 1♡! |
| 1♠ | 6♡ | All Pass | |

Johnnie Crawford opened hostilities with an out-and-out psychic 1♣ bid and this set Nils-Olof Lilliehook a small bidding problem. He could overcall 1◊ or 1NT, but both of these were un-newsworthy bids that might be found by a mere club player. No, it was clear to overcall 1♡ on the three-card suit. Howard Schenken showed no sense of occasion with his unimaginative response in spades and Gunnar Anulf leapt directly to a small slam. (Nowadays, players might have invoked Exclusion Roman Key-card Blackwod on his hand, leaping to 5♣ to ask for key cards outside the club suit.)

South was less terrified by a raise to six than East would have been. He did, after all, hold three trump honours. The slam would have had no play on a spade lead. East would ruff and return a diamond to receive a second ruff for two down. (Note that a Lightner double was not a possibility for East, since spades was his partner's suit.) Had Howard Schenken begun with the ◊A, the sight of dummy would probably have led him to find the spade continuation, scuttling the contract. His partner might have offered direction by following with a suit-preference ◊J. No, Schenken opted for the God-given lead in clubs and who can blame him?

Not to be outdone on such a psychic-dominated deal, Schenken led specifically the ♣A, which denied the king in their system. Declarer ruffed in the dummy, crossed to his ♡A and played the ♣J. Unsure whether his opening-lead psychic had been exposed, Schenken did not cover. Now Lilliehook was home. He discarded dummy's ◊K, overtook the ♡J with the queen and led a low spade towards his hand. East would not gain by ruffing a loser, so he discarded. South won with the ♠Q and led back the ♠10. When this was covered by the jack, he played low from dummy. He was subsequently able to ruff a spade, setting up the suit, and that was 1430 on his score-card a solid gain of 780 points against the 5♡ achieved by the Americans at the other table. Looking back at the diagram, who would imagine that declarer had made 6♡, losing just one trick to the ♠J?

# 12
# Cardinal Sins:
# Ruffing Partner's Winner

**T**hou shalt not ruff partner's winner' is pretty high on the list of Bridge Commandments, only a place or two below the sound guideline: 'Thou shalt not murder thy partner.' A cartoon featured in *Bridge Plus* magazine showed a tombstone that was engraved:

> *Here lie the bones of Afred Skinner*
> *who'd always ruff his partner's winner*

Presumably the gentleman was in the habit of ruffing his partners' winners and met with a violent death at the hands of some irate sufferer. Call us soft-hearted liberals but we consider execution too harsh a punishment for this crime. Particularly when it is the only way to beat the contract.

Many players are reluctant to ruff their partner's winners even when it is manifestly the winning move. The following deal was reported originally by Barry Rigal from a US National Championship:

---

**Dealer: South. North-South Vulnerable.**

|  | ♠ K 6 3 |  |
|---|---|---|
|  | ♡ K J 10 3 |  |
|  | ◇ A 8 |  |
|  | ♣ K 5 4 3 |  |

| ♠ 9 | | ♠ A 10 8 7 4 |
| ♡ Q | | ♡ 7 6 2 |
| ◇ Q 9 6 5 2 | | ◇ J 10 7 4 |
| ♣ A Q 8 7 6 2 | | ♣ 10 |

|  | ♠ Q J 5 2 |  |
|---|---|---|
|  | ♡ A 9 8 5 4 |  |
|  | ◇ K 3 |  |
|  | ♣ J 9 |  |

| West | North | East | South |
|------|-------|------|-------|
|  |  |  | 1♡ |
| 2NT | 4♡ | All Pass |  |

---

West, who had shown the minor suits with his 2NT intervention, led the
♠9 against game in hearts. East won with the ♠A and could tell that his
partner's lead was a likely singleton. Since four tricks were needed to
beat the game, he returned the ♣10 rather than give partner an
immediate spade ruff. South covered with the jack and West won with
the ace.

Can you imagine how the contract survived this bright start by the
defenders? West 'cleverly' returned the ♣Q, having calculated that this
would pin South's ♣9. No damage would have been done if declarer had
covered with dummy's king. East would have ruffed and delivered a
spade ruff to defeat the contract. South was a tricky customer, however.
Matching one clever move (ahem) with another, he played low in the
dummy. Since the queen was a winner, East saw no need to ruff. He held
his fire, planning to ruff the next club. This was not one of the world's
best-laid plans. The defenders had scored the first three tricks but there
was now no way to add to this total. The chance of a spade ruff by West
had been lost.

Where do you place the blame for this horror? West's play of the ♣Q
was a pointless move that gave his partner a chance to go wrong. It
should have been entirely obvious to him that it was East who held the
singleton club. Otherwise he would have delivered a spade ruff
immediately. So, one black mark to West. What about his partner? Was
he blameless? If West did hold only five clubs, leaving declarer with
three, East had nothing to lose by ruffing partner's winner anyway! West
could then deliver a second club ruff after ruffing the spade return.

In the rest of this chapter the defenders did not shirk their duty when
it came to ruffing partner's winner. As always, we will concentrate on
how they were able to detect that it was the right thing to do. Our first
exhibit comes from the Open Pairs event of the 1996 China Cup:

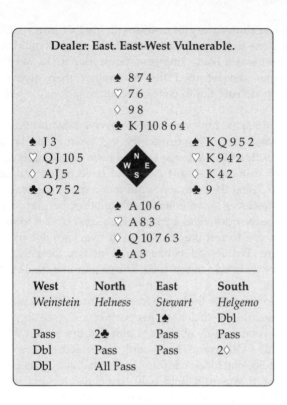

Dealer: East. East-West Vulnerable.

```
                    ♠ 8 7 4
                    ♡ 7 6
                    ◇ 9 8
                    ♣ K J 10 8 6 4
   ♠ J 3                              ♠ K Q 9 5 2
   ♡ Q J 10 5          N              ♡ K 9 4 2
   ◇ A J 5          W     E           ◇ K 4 2
   ♣ Q 7 5 2           S              ♣ 9
                    ♠ A 10 6
                    ♡ A 8 3
                    ◇ Q 10 7 6 3
                    ♣ A 3
```

| West | North | East | South |
|------|-------|------|-------|
| *Weinstein* | *Helness* | *Stewart* | *Helgemo* |
| | | 1♠ | Dbl |
| Pass | 2♣ | Pass | Pass |
| Dbl | Pass | Pass | 2◇ |
| Dbl | All Pass | | |

Fred Stewart opened 1♠ and Geir Helgemo doubled with the South cards (not exactly a textbook double, but experts make their own rules). You may have doubts about the pass-then-double method employed by West, too. What was wrong with a redouble on his hand? East-West can make ten tricks in hearts, so defending 2♣ doubled would not be such a triumph, even if they did manage to get it one down.

Contrary to general appearances, Helgemo cannot see through the backs of the cards. Unaware of his partner's fine club suit, he decided to try his luck in 2◇. Steve Weinstein doubled this contract too and led the ♠J. Declarer won with the ace and ducked a round of hearts. Weinstein played low since he wanted partner to win the trick and play a trump through South. This duly happened and Weinstein won with the jack, cashed the ace of trumps and played his remaining spade.

East won with the ♠Q and continued with the ♠K. West knew that it was urgent to drive out South's ♡A, before a discard could be taken on dummy's club suit. Afraid that partner might continue with a fourth spade, Weinstein ruffed his partner's winning ♠K and played a heart himself going out of his way to make things easy for partner. Declarer won the heart switch and played the ♣A and a club to the jack. East ruffed with the king and cashed a heart for two down.

On the next deal the defenders ruffed each other's winners no fewer than three times. Was it some husband and wife couple, whose marriage was on the verge of a break-up? No, it was Holland's Piet Jansen and Jan Westerhof, competing in the Open Teams at the Vilamoura European Championships in 1995.

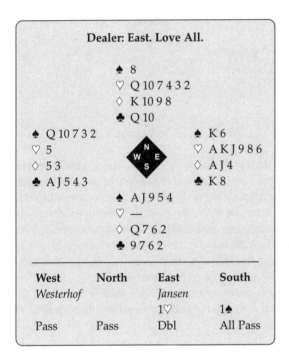

**Dealer: East. Love All.**

|  | ♠ 8 |  |
|---|---|---|
|  | ♡ Q 10 7 4 3 2 |  |
|  | ◇ K 10 9 8 |  |
|  | ♣ Q 10 |  |
| ♠ Q 10 7 3 2 |  | ♠ K 6 |
| ♡ 5 |  | ♡ A K J 9 8 6 |
| ◇ 5 3 |  | ◇ A J 4 |
| ♣ A J 5 4 3 |  | ♣ K 8 |
|  | ♠ A J 9 5 4 |  |
|  | ♡ — |  |
|  | ◇ Q 7 6 2 |  |
|  | ♣ 9 7 6 2 |  |

| West | North | East | South |
|---|---|---|---|
| *Westerhof* |  | *Jansen* |  |
|  |  | 1♡ | 1♠ |
| Pass | Pass | Dbl | All Pass |

West(erhof) led his singleton heart and declarer ruffed. After a diamond to the king and ace, East switched to the ♠K. The standard switch from such a holding would be the ♠6, forcing declarer to play something high on a mere spot-card. Here Jansen was hoping that his partner's trumps were strong and that king and another trump would seriously damage declarer's holding.

Declarer won with the ♠A, cashed the ◇Q and conceded a diamond to East's jack, West throwing a club. Jansen might have played another trump now, but he cashed the ♣K and led a high heart. Declarer threw a club from his hand and Westerhof ruffed his partner's heart winner with the ♠3. Unless he reduced his trumps, he would have to ruff later and lead a trump into South's tenace. Westerhof cashed the ♣A to leave:

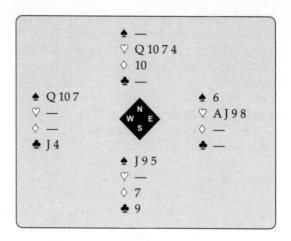

West led the master ♣J and it was East's turn to ruff his partner's winner. (Had he left his partner on lead, West would have had to exit with a club, ruffed by South, and then ruff a diamond to concede a further trump trick to declarer.) The ♡A came next, declarer discarding a diamond. The defenders would now make 500, for three down, even if West discarded. Just for fun, he ruffed his partner's winner yet again and exited with a club, collecting the last two tricks with the ♠Q-10. You can think of the deal as a triple Grand Coup in defence!

In our next example from an eight-table event some players didn't dare commit the sin, some went for it, while others pulled their partners away from it:

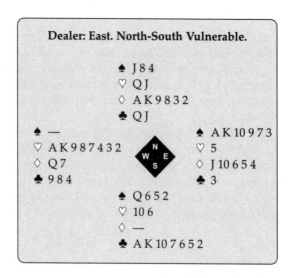

*Bridge Hands to Make You Laugh . . . and Cry*

The wild deal comes from the final holding of the late and much lamented *Macallan* tournament. Game in hearts cannot be made (unless playing against close relatives) but most Souths went to 5♣ and were doubled there. Will this phantom sacrifice cost 500 or 800, do you think?

At one table Honjun Xu of China led the ♡A and ♡K against 5♣. Zejun Zhuang, sitting East, ruffed the king without a flicker and played three rounds of spades. This gave the Chinese five tricks for +800.

At another table, Omar Sharif was West; he also led the ♡A but when his partner Christian Mari followed with the five, a clear singleton by their methods, Omar switched to the ♡9, forcing partner to ruff and switch to spades.

Just in case you scoff at going to such lengths to make things clearer for one's partner, see what happened at the table where Tony Forrester led the ♡A and ♡K against the same contract. His partner failed to ruff (it's only fair to say that it was not Andrew Robson) and they collected only 500.

Although Omar Sharif was keen to spare his partner from the path of sin on that deal, he is known to have committed the sin himself. He sat West on this deal from the 1998 *Generali* Masters, an individual tournament for invited experts only:

```
                 Dealer: South. Love All.

                   ♠ 5 2
                   ♡ K Q 8 6
                   ◇ A K Q 9
                   ♣ K J 7
  ♠ Q                              ♠ A K J 10 7 4 3
  ♡ 9 5             N              ♡ 4 3
  ◇ 10 8 4 2     W     E           ◇ J 6 3
  ♣ A Q 10 9 6 5     S             ♣ 8
                   ♠ 9 8 6
                   ♡ A J 10 7 2
                   ◇ 7 5
                   ♣ 4 3 2
```

| West | North | East | South |
|------|-------|------|-------|
| *Sharif* | *Mouiel* | *Jourdain* | *Kowalski* |
| | | | Pass |
| Pass | 1◇ | 3♠ | Pass |
| Pass | Dbl | Pass | 4♡ |
| All Pass | | | |

Sharif led his singleton ♠Q, Patrick Jourdain overtaking and firing back his singleton club. Omar won and gave him his ruff. East continued with the ♠10, which South could not cover. Sharif now committed the sin, ruffing his partner's winner to give him another club ruff. This excellent defence achieved two down, for plus 100, but it turned out to be a below average score for Sharif. Can you guess why?

At no fewer than seven tables West opened 3♣ and North overcalled 3NT. East was charmed to see the ♠Q appear under his ♠A lead. He proceeded to cash seven spades, followed by a club, obtaining the magic 200. It seems that in Sharif's case, sin had to be its own reward.

So, next time your partner ruffs your winner don't rush to yell at him. It might, just possibly, be a brilliant move. If he does it consistently or happens to ruff your ace with the ace of trumps . . . you could fax him the cartoon of Mr Skinner's tombstone!

HERE LIE

THE BONES OF

**ALFRED SKINNER**

WHO'D ALWAYS RUFF

HIS PARTNER'S

WINNER

# 13
# Confession is Good for the Soul

We have always admired players who tell stories against themselves. Hats off, then, to Hugh Ross, who reported this story to the Bulletin editors at the 1999 Vancouver NABC (North American Bridge Championship). "I blew 600 with my lead at Trick 1 and another 1170 with my lead at Trick 2," he told them. This was the deal:

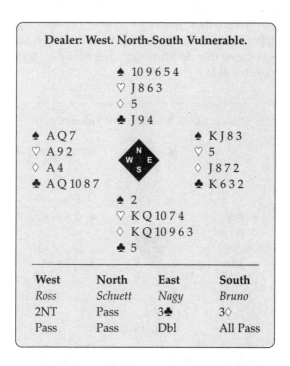

Dealer: West. North-South Vulnerable.

```
                    ♠ 10 9 6 5 4
                    ♡ J 8 6 3
                    ◇ 5
                    ♣ J 9 4
   ♠ A Q 7                        ♠ K J 8 3
   ♡ A 9 2              N         ♡ 5
   ◇ A 4            W     E       ◇ J 8 7 2
   ♣ A Q 10 8 7        S         ♣ K 6 3 2
                    ♠ 2
                    ♡ K Q 10 7 4
                    ◇ K Q 10 9 6 3
                    ♣ 5
```

| West | North | East | South |
|------|-------|------|-------|
| *Ross* | *Schuett* | *Nagy* | *Bruno* |
| 2NT | Pass | 3♣ | 3◇ |
| Pass | Pass | Dbl | All Pass |

Note that 6♣ (or even 7♣) is cold for East-West but difficult to bid. A sound alternative was to double 3◇. On a black-suit lead and continuation, South would lose control, scoring just five trump tricks for a penalty of 1100. What opening lead would you have made?

Hugh Ross led the ◇A, which left declarer in control of the hand. The maximum penalty now available was only 500, so the opening lead had cost 600. How would you have continued at Trick 2?

Not wishing to assist declarer in the side suits, Ross played another trump. Declarer now lost one trick in each suit, making 3◇ doubled for +670. Another 1170 points had been blown. They say that confession is good for the soul. Hugh Ross's soul must be in top-class shape.

# 14
# The Bargain You Can Ill Afford

Your opponents bid 'too high' at both tables. Is that good news? If both contracts are beaten, it will be a small swing your way. If one contract is allowed to sneak home, you may lose a sizable swing. If both contracts are allowed to make . . . not only is the adverse swing even more enormous but you may find that your deal is written up in Chapter 14 of some book by Bird and Sarantakos.

We will start with a deal from the Round of 16 at the 2000 Olympiad in Maastricht. With sixteen boards to play, England trailed Belgium by 38 IMPs. They overcame this deficit to win eventually by 5 IMPs, helped substantially by this deal:

```
           Dealer: North. North-South Vulnerable.

                      ♠ —
                      ♡ K 10 9 5 4
                      ◇ A 9 6 4 2
                      ♣ J 4 3
      ♠ A 6 4 3              N          ♠ Q J 10 8 7 2
      ♡ A J 8 7         W         E     ♡ —
      ◇ Q 8 7                S          ◇ J 10 3
      ♣ A 7                             ♣ Q 10 8 5
                      ♠ K 9 5
                      ♡ Q 6 3 2
                      ◇ K 5
                      ♣ K 9 6 2
```

| West | North | East | South |
|------|-------|------|-------|
| Hallberg | van Middelem | Simpson | Engel |
| | Pass | 2♠ | Pass |
| 4♠ | All Pass | | |

Cover all the hands except South's for the moment and try to dismiss the other hands from your mind. Now, what would you lead against 4♠?

The Belgian South's choice was a heart and that was the end for the defence. Declarer was able to ruff the heart lead and pick up the trump suit. It was not even necessary to guess correctly in clubs, since one club could be discarded on the ♡A and another could be ruffed in dummy. Declarer lost just two diamonds and a club.

The ◇K was the only lead to defeat 4♠. The defenders can then take two diamonds and a diamond ruff, eventually scoring the setting trick in clubs. Should South find this lead? A doubleton honour is not usually an attractive lead. For every time that it is a spectacular success (as here), there will be three or four deals where it gives declarer the contract. There were two pointers towards the lead on this particular deal. Firstly, there was no attractive lead elsewhere. A trump lead was probably safe but a lead in any of the three side suits might work out poorly. A second reason to lead a diamond was that South held K-x-x in the trump suit. Even if partner did not hold the ◇A, there might be a second chance to get a ruff when he won with the ♠K.

Having said all that, at the fifteen tables where East played in 4♠ only four defenders led the ◇K. Among them were Geir Helgemo and Alexander Dubinin, the respective South players in the Norway *vs* Russia encounter. An honourable push!

In the Closed Room of the England-Belgium encounter, there was a twist:

| West | North | East | South |
|------|-------|------|-------|
| *Labaere* | *Liggins* | *Carcassonne* | *Fawcett* |
| | Pass | 2♠ | Pass |
| 4♠ | Dbl | Pass | 4NT |
| Dbl | 5◇ | Pass | 5♡ |
| Dbl | All Pass | | |

Glyn Liggins was the odd man out, the sole North who refused to be shut out. Perhaps emboldened by the 38-IMP deficit, he doubled 4♠ for take-out and unearthed the heart fit for his side. The Belgian West doubled, of course, but Liggins had right-sided the contract and Alain Labaere was end-played to some extent at Trick 1. Applying 'least of evils' logic, he launched the defence with the ♠A. Liggins ruffed in the dummy and played a heart to the queen and ace, East showing out. All depended on West's next play. You have seen all four hands, of course, but what do you think you would have played next, sitting West?

West opted for aggression and switched to ace and another club. Disaster! Liggins won the second round of clubs with the king. He was then able to finesse twice in trumps, nullifying West's holding, and to ruff the diamonds good. That was +850 and a 15-IMP swing to England.

What did you make of that club switch? If your sole aim is to beat the contract, the switch cannot be justified. Since your trump length matches declarer's, he will not be able to set up the diamond suit, discard clubs from his hand and ruff clubs there. So, if your partner does hold the ♣K the defenders' tricks in the suit cannot disappear. If instead declarer holds the ♣K, then a club switch could prove very expensive. You do better to exit passively and wait for whatever club tricks Fate will give you. It seems that the only reason to switch to a club is that you will score a ruff, for two down, when partner does hold the ♣K.

In theory the English overbid in both rooms and were slated to lose 6 IMPs. In practice they won 15 IMPs and the match with it. Teams sometimes console themselves when on a particular board they have a bad result at both tables. "It would have cost much more if we had a bad result on two different boards," they say. That's true in a way. Instead of two disasters each costing around 12 IMPs, you get two disasters for the bargain price of just 15 IMPs. Mind you, a team can ill afford too many such bargains. In this case the Belgians lost a bushel of points on the remaining deals of the set, which may be partly attributed to the psychological shock suffered here.

The next 'double disaster' deal arose in the European Mixed Teams Championship of 2000, played in Rimini. Chemla beat Labaere (yes, the same guy who featured on the previous deal) by a slight margin, thanks to this board:

**Dealer: West. North-South Vulnerable.**

|  | ♠ Q J 9 8 7 4 3 |  |
|---|---|---|
|  | ♡ 7 |  |
|  | ◇ 8 7 |  |
|  | ♣ 7 6 4 |  |
| ♠ A 10 |  | ♠ K 6 5 2 |
| ♡ K J 10 8 6 2 |  | ♡ Q 9 5 4 |
| ◇ Q 3 2 |  | ◇ A K 6 5 |
| ♣ J 5 |  | ♣ 2 |
|  | ♠ — |  |
|  | ♡ A 3 |  |
|  | ◇ J 10 9 4 |  |
|  | ♣ A K Q 10 9 8 3 |  |

| West | North | East | South |
|---|---|---|---|
| *van* | *Favas* | *van den* | *Quantin* |
| *Middelem* |  | *Bossche* |  |
| 1♡ | Pass | 1♠ | 5♣ |
| Pass | Pass | Dbl | All Pass |

The East hand appears to be a text-book definition of a 4♣ splinter bid. The Belgian East thought that little damage could come from a gentle exploration and responded with a 'scientific' 1♠. She must have regretted this a few moments later, when the bidding returned to her at the level of 5♣! She elected to double, which was a close decision when she had not told partner of her excellent heart support. West led the ♠A, ruffed by declarer, and a diamond was played to the eight and king. What should East do next?

A trump switch would ensure the defeat of the contract because West could win the second round of diamonds with the queen. With dummy's spades looking a threat, East took the view that the defenders needed to cash two more tricks in the red suits. A heart switch would not have been fatal but East continued with a disastrous ◇A. A trump switch is no good now because one diamond ruff will bring down West's queen and dummy will still have a trump for a heart ruff. When East in fact switched to the ♡Q, declarer won with the ace and lost no further trick. +750 for the French team.

Some critics claimed at the time that West should have led a trump. Oh yes? Trump leads are more often diagnosed in the post-mortem than at the table. There was no reason at all to expect ruffing values in the dummy when West held two trumps and East had doubled 5♣. Ace and another spade, possibly to be followed by a trump promotion, was a tempting defence indeed. We divide the blame equally between East's ◇A play and her earlier bid of 1♠!

This was the bidding at the other table:

| West | North | East | South |
|------|-------|------|-------|
| *Chemla* | *Carcassonne* | *D'Ovidio* | *Labaere* |
| 1♡ | Pass | 2◇ | 3NT |
| Pass | 4♠ | Dbl | 5♣ |
| Pass | Pass | 5♡ | Dbl |
| All Pass | | | |

If you want to make a waiting bid on those East cards, 2◇ is a more sensible effort than 1♠. The French East was understandably nervous of defending 5♣, with her unannounced heart support, and decided to install her partner in 5♡. As we see it, there was no indication at all for North to find the killing spade lead. She duly led a club and Chemla scored +650, to pick up 16 IMPs.

The records do not show which club was led. Suppose North-South were playing 'second best from bad suits' and North therefore led the ♣6. If South were to read her for ♣J-7-6, leaving South with ♣5-4, he might underplay with the ♣3. The aim would be to leave partner on lead to deliver a spade ruff! Not today and that would have been a doubled overtrick for the French team.

The next deal comes from the last holding in 2002 of the defunct *Forbo* tournament in the Netherlands. One of the local teams faced opposition from Bulgaria:

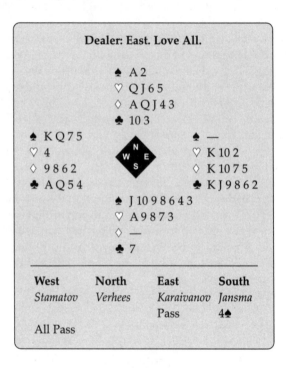

**Dealer: East. Love All.**

♠ A 2
♡ Q J 6 5
◇ A Q J 4 3
♣ 10 3

♠ K Q 7 5
♡ 4
◇ 9 8 6 2
♣ A Q 5 4

♠ —
♡ K 10 2
◇ K 10 7 5
♣ K J 9 8 6 2

♠ J 10 9 8 6 4 3
♡ A 9 8 7 3
◇ —
♣ 7

| West | North | East | South |
|------|-------|------|-------|
| *Stamatov* | *Verhees* | *Karaivanov* | *Jansma* |
| | | Pass | 4♠ |
| All Pass | | | |

What is the best action on those South cards? Since any given human player will have little experience of handling such hands, the answer can only be a guess. (It is the sort of question that can better be answered by a computer program. This could generate a thousand random deals from the remaining 39 cards, bid them and play them against various opening bids from South, and thereby calculate which opening bid is best.)

The Dutch South, a mere human, opted for 4♠, which was passed out. Even though a useful dummy was about to hit the table, all depended on West's opening lead. Only a club lead would beat the contract, since otherwise declarer could dispose of his club loser on the ◇A. Leading unsupported aces is not usually profitable and West very reasonably led his singleton heart. That was ten tricks and +420 for the Dutchmen.

The Dutch scored a game at the other table too:

| West | North | East | South |
|------|-------|------|-------|
| *Maas* | *Nanev* | *Ramondt* | *Mihov* |
| | | Pass | Pass |
| 1♣ | 1◊ | 2◊ | 2♠ |
| Pass | Pass | 5♣ | All Pass |

Once again, only the lead of an unsupported ace (here the ◊A) could beat the contract. If North leads the ♡Q, for example, declarer can cover with the king, to make sure that the safe hand wins the first trick. North preferred to lead the ace of his partner's suit and the Dutch had made beatable games at both tables for a 13-IMP gain. Since we were not able to find fault with the two (costly) opening leads, the main message appears to be that it pays to bid up!

In our next example, one team makes a game at one table and is doubled into a making game at the other table. It happened in the first round of the 2001 Vanderbilt, when a ladies team laden with world champions faced a talented team of fearless juniors:

### Dealer: East. Both Vulnerable.

```
                  ♠ 9 7
                  ♡ A 4 2
                  ◊ A Q J 8 3
                  ♣ K 10 7
  ♠ A Q J 6                    ♠ 8 5 2
  ♡ 3               N          ♡ J 10 7 6 5
  ◊ 6 4 2       W     E        ◊ 7
  ♣ 9 8 6 5 3       S          ♣ A Q J 4
                  ♠ K 10 4 3
                  ♡ K Q 9 8
                  ◊ K 10 9 5
                  ♣ 2
```

| West | North | East | South |
|------|-------|------|-------|
| *Chambers* | *Grue* | *Sutherlin* | *Wolpert* |
| | | Pass | 1◊ |
| 1♠ | 2♣ | 3♠ | 4◊ |
| Pass | 4♡ | Pass | 5◊ |
| All Pass | | | |

Would you open that South hand, in the second seat? Both South players did and, indeed, it seems to be part of the modern game to open such hands. Terence Reese used to argue that a 4-4-4-1 shape was good for defending, rather than declaring. Apart from that, if you open 1◊ you will have no easy rebid if partner responds 2♣. Nor will you necessarily be advising partner of a good opening lead, should the enemy win the auction. As we see it, these are three good reasons for not opening.

West overcalled 1♠, again at both tables, and we have some admiration for this bid. It kills the expected 1♡ response from North and may suggest a good lead for partner. It may also deter the opponents from bidding a makeable 3NT. North cue-bid 2♠ to show at least a limit raise in diamonds and the spotlight turned to East. We don't like the 3♠ bid on three small trumps. She didn't want a spade lead and if North-South subsided in 3◊, she could compete in spades later. The juniors duly bid 5◊ and, solely because of East's raise in spades, West let the game through with a disastrous ♠A lead. This was the auction at the other table:

| West | North | East | South |
|------|-------|------|-------|
| Wooldridge | Molson | Campbell | Sokolow |
| | | Pass | 1◊ |
| 1♠ | 2♠ | 3♠ | Pass |
| Pass | Dbl | All Pass | |

North competed with a double on the second round and Tobi Sokolow passed this for penalties, hoping for a club ruff or two. North led the ♠9 to declarer's queen and a diamond was conceded. North won and continued with the ♠7, covered by the eight, ten and jack. Declarer could now cross to the ♣Q and take a successful finesse of the ♠6! Nine black-suit tricks gave him +730 and a swing of 16 IMPs.

Did you see how the contract could have been defeated? Obviously heart forces would work well, but this was difficult to diagnose. No, there was a defence even after North had made those two trump leads. When the ♠7 is covered by dummy's ♠8, South must play low from K-10-4! Declarer can pick up the trumps with a finesse of the jack, yes, but he can finesse only once in clubs now. He cannot pick up the suit.

We end with the ultimate double disaster, a beatable grand slam made by the opponents at both tables! We have to dip deep into bridge history to find such a happening. Victor Mollo describes the following deal, played in Stockholm in the 1950s, in his splendid book *Bridge Immortals*:

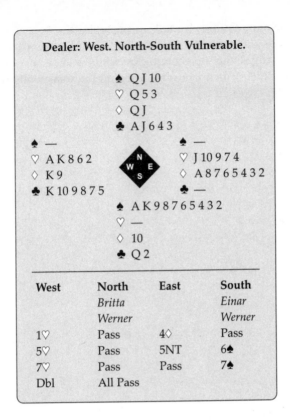

**Dealer: West. North-South Vulnerable.**

```
              ♠ Q J 10
              ♡ Q 5 3
              ◇ Q J
              ♣ A J 6 4 3
♠ —                         ♠ —
♡ A K 8 6 2                 ♡ J 10 9 7 4
◇ K 9                       ◇ A 8 7 6 5 4 3 2
♣ K 10 9 8 7 5              ♣ —
              ♠ A K 9 8 7 6 5 4 3 2
              ♡ —
              ◇ 10
              ♣ Q 2
```

| West | North | East | South |
|------|-------|------|-------|
|      | *Britta* |   | *Einar* |
|      | *Werner* |   | *Werner* |
| 1♡   | Pass  | 4◇   | Pass  |
| 5♡   | Pass  | 5NT  | 6♠    |
| 7♡   | Pass  | Pass | 7♠    |
| Dbl  | All Pass |   |       |

East's 4◇ was a Culbertson asking bid. Einar Werner decided to lie low for a round or two and West's 5♡ response showed second-round diamond control plus the ♡A. 5NT was a grand slam force, asking partner to bid 7♡ if he held two of the three top trump honours. This was not particularly scientific, since West might bid the grand on a trump suit headed by the ace-queen. Nevertheless, East-West are to be commended on reaching the excellent grand on so few values.

Werner decided to sacrifice, expecting it to cost no more than 800. It did not turn out like that! West made the ill-advised lead of the ♡A. Surely the ◇K was a better shot, with East known to hold the ace of the suit? Werner ruffed and reeled off nine trumps squeezing West in clubs and hearts. The doubled grand slam was made for a score of +2420.

Does anything else occur to you – in particular, about the bidding? West had admitted to two heart honours, so North had a cast-iron double of the heart grand slam! Her ♡Q-x-x was a certain trick. Mind you, it was hard for her to predict that she needed to double in order to stop her passed-hand partner from sacrificing, vulnerable, at the seven level!

In the other room, Jan Wohlin and Nils Olof Lilliehook played in 7◇ doubled on the East-West cards. During the auction North had doubled

West's 5♣. South dutifully (but disastrously) led the ♣Q, covered by the king and ace and ruffed by East. Lilliehook drew trumps and ran the ♣10, eventually setting up enough club winners to dispose of his losing hearts. Plus 1580 was his reward, bringing the total swing to a round 4000.

# 15
# Defences From Hell!

In this chapter we will cast a sympathetic eye on some of the most awful defences ever perpetrated. Plenty to choose from, yes, but we will demand the very highest standard of awfulness – deals where an onlooker might study the diagram for some moments and say: "How could they possibly make that?" We will concentrate on how the defenders should have avoided the disaster. One of the most important ways to achieve a high standard in any game or sport is to learn from your mistakes. Here we will hope to learn from others' mistakes. The first horror deal comes from the 2003 Spring NABC in the USA:

**Dealer: West. Both Vulnerable.**

```
                ♠ 8765
                ♡ AJ62
                ◇ 83
                ♣ 732
  ♠ AJ932              ♠ Q4
  ♡ Q754        N      ♡ 83
  ◇ K2        W   E    ◇ AJ1097654
  ♣ 85          S      ♣ 9
                ♠ K10
                ♡ K109
                ◇ Q
                ♣ AKQJ1064
```

| West | North | East | South |
|------|-------|------|-------|
| Pass | Pass | 3◇ | 3NT |
| All Pass | | | |

Sitting South was Canadian star, Barry Harper. Although his singleton queen was not *guaranteed* to be a stopper in diamonds, he bid 3NT. There are many examples of declarer surviving with a stopper of Q-x because RHO ducked from A-K-x-x-x-x-x, hoping to maintain communications with his partner. In theory there is no reason why you should not score a singleton queen in this way. Also, of course, partner may put down some diamond bolster in the dummy. Can you imagine how 3NT was made after West led the ◇K?

---

East placed declarer with ◊Q-2 and West with a singleton king. In that case, very annoyingly, South's queen would stop the suit. To guide West with his switch, East followed suit with the ◊9 – a McKenney signal for spades. South produced the ◊Q and West was left on lead. What next? East-West's primary signalling method was 'reverse attitude', so from West's point of view a high card (such as the ◊9) was a discouraging signal in diamonds. Imagine East's sense of mounting horror as West considered his next move. East now knew, of course, that the ◊Q had been a singleton and that West held another diamond.

Eventually West concluded that his partner has pre-empted on six cards to the ace and that South had false-carded the queen from Q-J-x to encourage a continuation. He switched to a low spade and Barry Harper took the remaining tricks for +690. Declarer scored twelve tricks where the defenders could have taken the first eleven. ("A 23-trick swing!" claimed the daily bulletin, somewhat exaggerating the situation.)

How might the disaster have been avoided? Firstly, we don't like West's spade switch. Declarer was likely to hold solid clubs along with the ♡K. So, he could almost certainly run nine tricks if he gained the lead. If East did hold ♠K-x (alongside the expected ◊A-x-x-x-x-x), he could switch to spades himself at Trick 3, after the diamond position was exposed. West therefore had little to lose by playing another diamond. West was not the sole culprit, however. East should surely have overtaken the diamond king with the ace at Trick 1. If, as expected, the queen did not fall from declarer, he could then lead the ♠Q through declarer, beating the contract when South started with ♠K-3-2, ♠K-3 or ♠K-2.

We move next to the semi-finals of the 1989 Bermuda Bowl with Australia facing the USA:

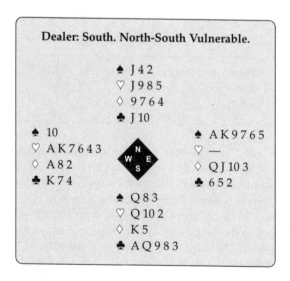

**Dealer: South. North-South Vulnerable.**

```
              ♠ J 4 2
              ♡ J 9 8 5
              ◊ 9 7 6 4
              ♣ J 10
  ♠ 10                      ♠ A K 9 7 6 5
  ♡ A K 7 6 4 3            ♡ —
  ◊ A 8 2          N        ◊ Q J 10 3
  ♣ K 7 4       W   E       ♣ 6 5 2
                   S
              ♠ Q 8 3
              ♡ Q 10 2
              ◊ K 5
              ♣ A Q 9 8 3
```

*Bridge Hands to Make You Laugh . . . and Cry*

| West | North | East | South |
|------|-------|------|-------|
| Lorentz | Stansby | Lester | Martel |
| | | | 1NT |
| | | | |
| Dbl | All Pass | | |

Game in either major would have been cold but the Australians could smell blood against the vulnerable weak 1NT. Gabi Lorentz led the ♡A and East discarded, showing spade values with his discard of the ♠9. Declarer, meanwhile, unblocked the ♡Q. When West switched to the ♠10, East had a tricky decision to make. To ensure +500 for two down, he must win the trick and switch to the ◇Q. This was by no means obvious, since if the spades in the closed hands were divided 2-2 it would be better to duck, preserving the spade link between the defenders' hands.

John Lester decided to play low on the spade switch and the trick was won with South's ♠Q. Declarer could have escaped for one down at this stage, by clearing the clubs and subsequently end-playing West for a sixth trick. The ♣K might have been onside, though, and Chip Martel instead led the ♡2. West ducked and dummy's ♡8 won. A key moment of the deal had been reached. When declarer ran the ♣J, the Australian West elected to win the trick. He was on lead in this position:

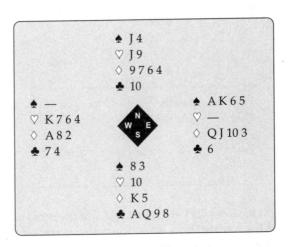

West cashed the ♡K and then needed to exit with a club to ensure one down. (Declarer could not then enjoy the ♡J and four club tricks.) No, West chose to play the ♡7. Declarer scored a second heart trick, followed by four club tricks, and the contract was made!

Look back at the end position and imagine that West had won the second club, leaving no club in the dummy. West could then play king

and another heart and declarer could not avoid 800 down. If West lets the
♣J win, the best declarer can do is to win the next club with the ace and
end-play West with a third club, but that is still 500 to the defenders.

When the deal was put to an expert panel in *Bridge World*, almost
everyone blamed West for the disaster, and most of them singled out the
♣K as the worst card played, although his ♡7 came close.

Have you ever made a small slam when missing K-Q-10-9-8 in the
trump suit? Italy's Dano de Falco achieved such a feat. Was he facing an
elderly married couple at his local club? No, he was up against the
mighty Brazilians, Gabriel Chagas and Marcelo Branco, in the round-
robin stage of the 1983 Bermuda Bowl. This was the deal:

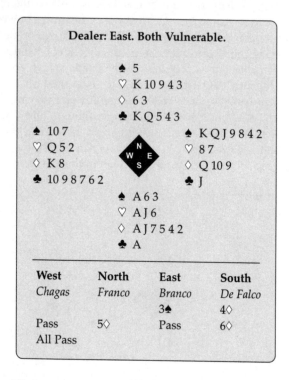

**Dealer: East. Both Vulnerable.**

|  | ♠ 5 |  |
|  | ♡ K 10 9 4 3 |  |
|  | ◇ 6 3 |  |
|  | ♣ K Q 5 4 3 |  |

| ♠ 10 7 | | ♠ K Q J 9 8 4 2 |
| ♡ Q 5 2 | | ♡ 8 7 |
| ◇ K 8 | | ◇ Q 10 9 |
| ♣ 10 9 8 7 6 2 | | ♣ J |

|  | ♠ A 6 3 |  |
|  | ♡ A J 6 |  |
|  | ◇ A J 7 5 4 2 |  |
|  | ♣ A |  |

| West | North | East | South |
|------|-------|------|-------|
| *Chagas* | *Franco* | *Branco* | *De Falco* |
|  |  | 3♠ | 4◇ |
| Pass | 5◇ | Pass | 6◇ |
| All Pass |  |  |  |

De Falco might have bid 3NT at his first turn. He preferred an overcall in
diamonds and advanced to a slam when this attracted a raise. An
unimpressive auction to an unimpressive contract! Chagas led the ♠10,
won with the ace, and the Italian declarer had to find some way to escape
for one trump loser. Unless a defender happened to hold K-Q doubleton,
his only chance was to persuade East to ruff a club from a three-card
trump holding.

De Falco cashed the ♣A and crossed to dummy with a spade ruff.
When he called for the ♣K Branco made the mistake of ruffing, with the

◇9. Declarer overruffed with the jack and, since the ruff had been from a three-card holding, he was part way towards making the contract. His next move was to play ace and another trump. Because Chagas held the king, and because he did not unblock the card under declarer's ace, it was he who won the second round of trumps. Unfortunately for his side, he had no spade to play. When he exited with a club, declarer won with dummy's queen, throwing his last spade, and crossed to his hand with a club ruff.

It may seem that declarer would still need to guess who held the ♡Q but de Falco demonstrated that this was not the case. He ran his remaining trumps, knowing that West would have to reduce to a doubleton heart in order to retain his club guard. The hearts then became the second five-card red suit to break 2-2! Declarer had his slam.

A splendid hand arose in the final of the very same Bermuda Bowl, that of 1983. The two big favourites, USA and Italy, were once again in opposition:

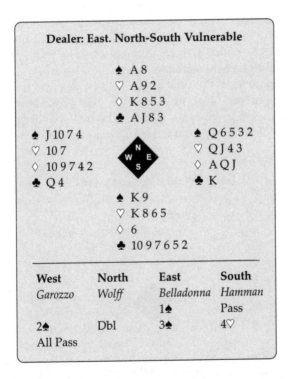

Dealer: East. North-South Vulnerable

|  | ♠ A 8 |  |
|  | ♡ A 9 2 |  |
|  | ◇ K 8 5 3 |  |
|  | ♣ A J 8 3 |  |

| ♠ J 10 7 4 |  | ♠ Q 6 5 3 2 |
| ♡ 10 7 |  | ♡ Q J 4 3 |
| ◇ 10 9 7 4 2 |  | ◇ A Q J |
| ♣ Q 4 |  | ♣ K |

|  | ♠ K 9 |  |
|  | ♡ K 8 6 5 |  |
|  | ◇ 6 |  |
|  | ♣ 10 9 7 6 5 2 |  |

| West | North | East | South |
|------|-------|------|-------|
| *Garozzo* | *Wolff* | *Belladonna* | *Hamman* |
|  |  | 1♠ | Pass |
| 2♠ | Dbl | 3♠ | 4♡ |
| All Pass |  |  |  |

At the other table Arturo Franco had made 5♣. He had ruffed out East's ◇A, setting up the ◇K, and cashed all his side-suit winners. He had then thrown West on lead with the ♣Q, forcing him to give a ruff-and-discard. Marvellously played, albeit with a fortunate lie of the cards, and the Italians had every reason to expect a game swing.

Playing in 4♡, Bob Hamman won the spade lead with the king and played a trump to the nine and jack. He won the spade return, cashed the ♡A and played a trump towards his hand. Although he had created an intra-finesse position it was pointless to finesse, because the spades were bare and the clubs had not yet been established. Realising that he needed a 3-3 trump break, Hamman went up with the ♡K. When West showed out, it seemed that five down vulnerable would be declarer's fate.

Hamman led the ♣10 and Garozzo covered with the queen! "Play the ace," said Hamman and . . . unbelievably, the king fell on his right. Benito Garozzo, rated by many as the world's top player, had crashed honours in defence. The game was now made, instead of going five down. The cover cost a net swing of 16 IMPs, more than three times the margin by which the Americans eventually won the championship.

Was it a clear-cut error to cover the ♣10? It seems so. If declarer held ♣K-10-9(-x-x) the cover would save him a guess. If he held ♣10-x-x(-x), he would surely not have led the ten in the first place. If declarer held ♣10-9-x(-x), a cover would make no difference. Only if declarer held ♣10-x would a cover save a trick. This holding was precluded because East was marked with 5-4 shape in the majors and could not therefore hold five of the seven outstanding clubs.

Before moving to the final (truly hellish) defence, let's look at a relatively humorous deal that arose in the 1998 *Generali* Masters Individual, played in Corsica's Ajaccio. The two current leaders in the tournament, Piotr Gawrys and Bobbie Richman, faced each other:

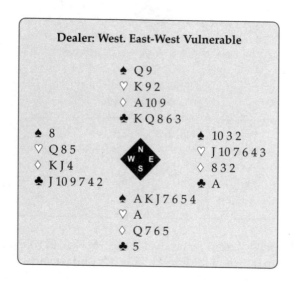

**Dealer: West. East-West Vulnerable**

```
              ♠ Q 9
              ♡ K 9 2
              ◇ A 10 9
              ♣ K Q 8 6 3
♠ 8                           ♠ 10 3 2
♡ Q 8 5          N            ♡ J 10 7 6 4 3
◇ K J 4      W       E        ◇ 8 3 2
♣ J 10 9 7 4 2       S        ♣ A
              ♠ A K J 7 6 5 4
              ♡ A
              ◇ Q 7 6 5
              ♣ 5
```

| West | North | East | South |
|------|-------|------|-------|
| *Hackett* | *Delmouly* | *Richman* | *Gawrys* |
| Pass | 1♣ | Pass | 2♠ |
| Pass | 2NT | Pass | 3♠ |
| Pass | 4◇ | Pass | 4NT |
| Pass | 5◇ | Pass | 6♠ |
| All Pass | | | |

Justin Hackett led the ♣J, covered by the king and ace. Consider it first as a defensive problem from the East seat. What would you return at Trick 2?

Your partner appears to hold length in clubs. He also holds whatever diamond protection the defence has and it follows that he might be subjected to a minor-suit squeeze. Since declarer holds only one club, a diamond return will break up the squeeze and legitimately beat the slam.

When Bobbie Richman returned a heart, declarer had a chance. The winning line is to cross to dummy's ♠Q, cash the ♡K and ruff a club. You then run the trumps and squeeze West in the minors. Gawrys decided to finesse dummy's ♠9 instead. By gaining an extra entry he would be able to set up and enjoy the clubs whenever they broke 4-3.

Gawrys boldly led a spade to the nine. Richman followed low, in sleep, and dummy's nine won. East showed out when a club was ruffed and Gawrys had to revert to the squeeze line anyway. West duly turned up with both minor-suit guards and the slam was made.

Only when Justin Hackett asked: "Why did you let the nine of spades win?" did Richman realise what he had done. Shaken by this disaster, he lost ground and eventually finished well down the field.

We will end the chapter with a deal from the 1988 Olympiad. New Zealand faced Canada and the two South players, fourth to speak, held four aces and four kings in their hand. Neither was in the least surprised when there was plenty of bidding before they had a chance to open:

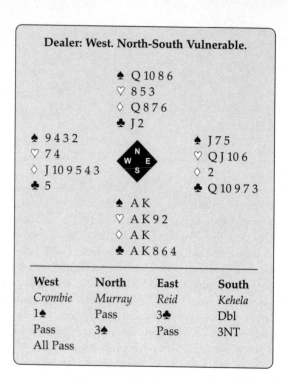

**Dealer: West. North-South Vulnerable.**

|  | ♠ Q 10 8 6 |  |
|---|---|---|
|  | ♡ 8 5 3 |  |
|  | ◊ Q 8 7 6 |  |
|  | ♣ J 2 |  |

| ♠ 9 4 3 2 | | ♠ J 7 5 |
|---|---|---|
| ♡ 7 4 | | ♡ Q J 10 6 |
| ◊ J 10 9 5 4 3 | | ◊ 2 |
| ♣ 5 | | ♣ Q 10 9 7 3 |

|  | ♠ A K |  |
|---|---|---|
|  | ♡ A K 9 2 |  |
|  | ◊ A K |  |
|  | ♣ A K 8 6 4 |  |

| West | North | East | South |
|---|---|---|---|
| *Crombie* | *Murray* | *Reid* | *Kehela* |
| 1♠ | Pass | 3♣ | Dbl |
| Pass | 3♠ | Pass | 3NT |
| All Pass | | | |

The New Zealand West opened 1♠. This was a 'Fert' bid, denoting 0-8 points and saying nothing about the spade suit. East's 3♣ was a gallant effort to take out as much bidding space as possible. This succeeded in a sense, because North-South stopped in game despite holding 33 points between them.

Even game proved to be a struggle. West led his singleton club to the ♣2, ♣9 and ♣K. Sami Kehela unblocked his two bare ace-king combinations and then played ace and another heart. East won with the ♡10 and returned the ♡Q to declarer's king. Kehela then threw East back on lead with a fourth round of hearts. For the moment it was safe to return the ♣Q, pinning dummy's ♣J. Kehela allowed the queen to hold, however, and now East had to surrender a ninth trick. He had to play a club, which would allow declarer to finesse the ♣8, or a spade to revive the dummy. Nine tricks made.

You are probably asking yourself: "What has that got to do with Defences from Hell?" We haven't told you what happened at the other table yet! The New Zealanders promoted themselves into 6NT:

| West | North | East | South |
|------|-------|------|-------|
| *Baran* | *Blackstock* | *Molson* | *Newell* |
| 3◊ | Pass | 3♡ | Dbl |
| Pass | 3♠ | Pass | 4◊ |
| Pass | 4♠ | Pass | 6NT |
| All Pass | | | |

Boris Baran followed the modern pre-emptive style and shunted the opponents into a no-play slam. Well, it should have been no-play but . . .

A heart was led and Peter Newell won with the ace. As at the other table, he then unblocked the two bare ace-king combinations, Mark Molson throwing a club. Declarer then led a club to the jack. He had no real hope of making the contract since even if West held ♣Q-x-x, he would be able to rise with the ♣Q, blocking the suit, and return a heart. Declarer would not then be able to enjoy dummy's two queens as well as his own long clubs. In fact the situation was even more bleak – the ♣J lost to East's ♣Q. These cards remained in play:

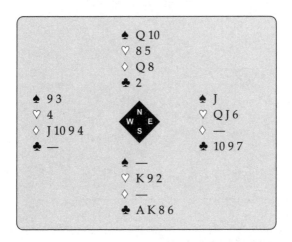

A seemingly obvious return of the ♡Q or ♣10 would have killed the slam. Molson had apparently not considered that declarer might have no entry to the dummy. Even though there could be no technical benefit from the play (so far as we can see), he returned the ♠J! Dummy's three winners were resurrected, lifting declarer's total from eight to eleven tricks. The last of dummy's winners also effected a squeeze on East, who had to surrender his guard in either hearts or clubs. 6NT had been made after a defence that had truly come from the depths of Hell!

# 16
# Just Enough to Double

The spectacular deal below was reported by Alfred Sheinwold in *Bridge World*. It was played in 1965 at the Cavendish Club:

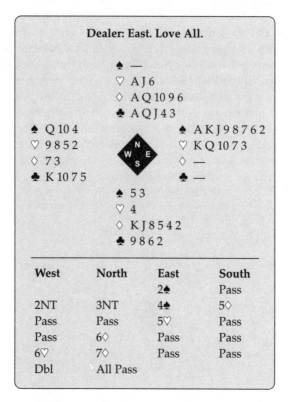

**Dealer: East. Love All.**

```
                    ♠ —
                    ♡ A J 6
                    ◇ A Q 10 9 6
                    ♣ A Q J 4 3
  ♠ Q 10 4                        ♠ A K J 9 8 7 6 2
  ♡ 9 8 5 2          N            ♡ K Q 10 7 3
  ◇ 7 3          W       E        ◇ —
  ♣ K 10 7 5         S            ♣ —
                    ♠ 5 3
                    ♡ 4
                    ◇ K J 8 5 4 2
                    ♣ 9 8 6 2
```

| West | North | East | South |
|------|-------|------|-------|
|      |       | 2♠   | Pass  |
| 2NT  | 3NT   | 4♠   | 5◇    |
| Pass | Pass  | 5♡   | Pass  |
| Pass | 6◇    | Pass | Pass  |
| 6♡   | 7◇    | Pass | Pass  |
| Dbl  | All Pass |   |       |

Since East had bid his spades twice before introducing the hearts, West might well have bid 6♠ instead of 6♡. In practice, South ended in 7◇ doubled. The declarer, Bea Gale, ruffed the spade lead, played a trump to the jack and casually advanced the ♣8. "Not through the Iron Duke," muttered Boris Koytchou, as he covered with the ♣10. Mrs Gale won with dummy's ♣Q, returned to her hand with a second round of trumps and led the ♣9, covered by the king and ace. The ♡A and a heart ruff allowed her to lead the ♣6, covered by the seven and jack. The setting trick was eventually claimed by West's ♣5.

"Give me the ♣4 instead of the ♣5 and I wouldn't have doubled!" observed West.

# 17
# Fortune Favours the Brave

They say that fortune favours the brave. Oh yes? It doesn't seem to happen when we overbid. In this chapter we will see some surprising deals where fortune did favour the brave. For example, one side bids game and makes it while the other side stops cautiously in a part-score and goes down. Or one side bids a slam and makes it; the other side plays safe, stopping in game, and goes down. You have the idea. We are looking for incongruous results between the two tables.

We will set our sights modestly, looking at a deal where game made and a partial failed. The deal is from the 2001 US team trials:

**Dealer: South. Love All.**

```
                    ♠ Q J 6 4
                    ♡ 8
                    ◊ A J 9 5 4 3
                    ♣ 8 3
    ♠ A K 9 3 2                      ♠ 10 5
    ♡ 7 4 3 2            N           ♡ 10 6
    ◊ Q              W       E       ◊ K 7 6 2
    ♣ K 6 2              S           ♣ Q 10 9 5 4
                    ♠ 8 7
                    ♡ A K Q J 9 5
                    ◊ 10 8
                    ♣ A J 7
```

| West | North | East | South |
|------|-------|------|-------|
| *Rodwell* | *Ekeblad* | *Meckstroth* | *Lipsitz* |
| | | | 1♡ |
| 1♠ | Pass | Pass | 3♡ |
| All Pass | | | |

Eric Rodwell cashed the ♠A-K and then switched to his singleton ◊Q. As the cards lay, this was very much the right card to play, killing the entry to dummy's spade winners. Robert Lipsitz won with the ace and tried to cash the ♠Q. Suppose you had been East. Would you have ruffed with the ♡10 or the ♡6?

In many situations it would be right to attempt an uppercut, ruffing

---

with the ♡10. This might well knock a hole in declarer's trump holding, promoting a trump trick for West. It's a tempting defence but it would have given away the contract here. Declarer could have overruffed with an honour and crossed to dummy with the promoted ♡8! Since this would also draw East's last trump, he could then have taken a discard on the ♠J.

Jeff Meckstroth made no such mistake. He ruffed with the ♡6 and the contract was doomed. Declarer overruffed with the ♡9 but could not avoid an eventual five losers in the side suits. One down.

This was the auction at the other table:

| West | North | East | South |
|------|-------|------|-------|
| *Granovetter* | *Freeman* | *Rubin* | *Nickell* |
| | | | 1♡ |
| 1♠ | 3◊ | Pass | 4♡ |
| All Pass | | | |

North's 3◊ response was a 'weak jump shift' but this was enough to encourage Nick Nickell to bid the game. Matthew Granovetter cashed the ♠A and ♠K, as at the other table. What should he do next, would you say?

As the cards lay, Granovetter could beat the heart game either by continuing spades (allowing partner to ruff one of dummy's winners) or by driving out dummy's entry in diamonds. When he switched to a low club instead, Nickell won with the ace and drew trumps. He could then cross to the ◊A and throw his two club losers on the ♠Q and ♠J.

Time to move to the next deal? Of course not! To get the maximum benefit from these deals we must study the defence at the two tables and decide whether the participants should have done better. Meckstroth and Granovetter are both world-class players. Why did one switch to a diamond, whereas the other switched to a club? The answer is that they were defending different contracts! They each had to work out the best chance of scoring the number of tricks that they needed. At Granovetter's table the contract could be beaten if he could find East with the ♣A. Since South had leapt to game after hearing of the weak response in diamonds, it was perhaps more likely that declarer held the ◊K rather than the ♣A. At any rate, Granovetter had to guess which of these cards East held and he guessed wrongly.

Let's look at the other table now. Finding East with the ♣A would not beat the lower contract of 3♡. West could tell from his 7-4-3-2 in the trump suit that declarer would be able to draw trumps and claim the remainder after four black-suit tricks had been taken. So, at his table the only real chance of beating the contract was to switch to diamonds, hoping to remove the entry to dummy. As we see it, neither West player did anything wrong. As happens a few million times every day, luck played a role in the outcome of the hand. Fortune favoured the brave on this occasion.

Next we will look for a deal where game made but a two-level part-score went down. It happened at the 2002 European Championships, with Norway facing Poland:

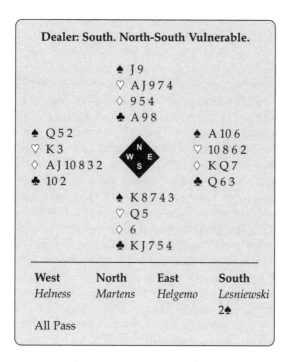

Dealer: South. North-South Vulnerable.

♠ J 9
♡ A J 9 7 4
♢ 9 5 4
♣ A 9 8

♠ Q 5 2          ♠ A 10 6
♡ K 3            ♡ 10 8 6 2
♢ A J 10 8 3 2   ♢ K Q 7
♣ 10 2           ♣ Q 6 3

♠ K 8 7 4 3
♡ Q 5
♢ 6
♣ K J 7 5 4

| West | North | East | South |
|------|-------|------|-------|
| *Helness* | *Martens* | *Helgemo* | *Lesniewski* |
| | | | 2♠ |
| All Pass | | | |

Marcin Lesniewski opened with a Polish two-bid, showing around 5-9 points and a major-minor two-suiter, and was left to play there. Tor Helness led the ♡K, which was apparently a favourable lead for declarer. (Indeed, ten tricks can be made by playing a trump to the king and a second trump. When declarer regains the lead he plays a third trump and loses just two trumps and one diamond.) It seems that Lesniewski's concentration dropped. He played ace, king and another club, without first cashing the ♡Q. West was quick to discard his last heart and the part-score could no longer be made.

At the other table the Norwegian North-South set their sights higher – too high, most would say.

| West | North | East | South |
|------|-------|------|-------|
| Balicki | Brogeland | Zmudzinski | Saelensminde |
| | | | 1♠ |
| 2◇ | Dbl | 2NT | 3♣ |
| Pass | 3◇ | Dbl | 4♣ |
| Pass | 4♠ | All Pass | |

World-class experts open lighter than club players. We realise that, yes, but a one-bid on an aceless 9-count including a doubleton queen? Let's accept it for the moment. West overcalls 2◇, partner doubles and East bids 2NT. Would you bid again on the South cards? Erik Saelensminde had in mind that his partner would not expect too much because he had not doubled 2NT. It's a fair point but, at the risk of being regarded as two old fogies, we humbly suggest that South did not have a 3♣ rebid!

The 'obvious' weakness of the South hand was not apparent to North. He cue-bid 3◇ and a few moments later Saelensminde found himself in 4♠ on a miserable 5-2 fit with only 19 points between the hands. West led the ◇A and continued the suit, shortening declarer's trumps. Saelensminde led the ♡Q, covered by the king and ace, and then ran the jack of trumps to West's queen. Cezary Balicki continued his attack in diamonds. Declarer had to ruff and was now down to two trumps, the same number as both West and East. He crossed to dummy with a second round of hearts and led a trump towards the king. East rose with the trump ace but had no further diamond to play. When the club finesse was right too (Fortune was truly lavishing her attention on the brave here), Saelensminde had ten tricks.

Do you see the chance that the defenders missed at this table? When the jack of trumps was led on the first round, East should have risen with the ace and forced declarer with his last diamond. If declarer had then played king and another trump (hoping that East had started with A-Q-x in the suit), West would have won and scored the rest of his diamond suit.

The next deal decided the France-China quarter-final in the 1995 Beijing world championship:

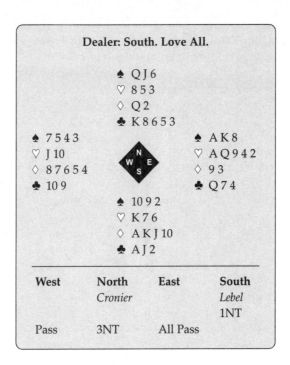

**Dealer: South. Love All.**

|  |  |  |
|---|---|---|
| | ♠ Q J 6 | |
| | ♡ 8 5 3 | |
| | ◇ Q 2 | |
| | ♣ K 8 6 5 3 | |
| ♠ 7 5 4 3 | | ♠ A K 8 |
| ♡ J 10 | | ♡ A Q 9 4 2 |
| ◇ 8 7 6 5 4 | | ◇ 9 3 |
| ♣ 10 9 | | ♣ Q 7 4 |
| | ♠ 10 9 2 | |
| | ♡ K 7 6 | |
| | ◇ A K J 10 | |
| | ♣ A J 2 | |

| West | North | East | South |
|---|---|---|---|
| | *Cronier* | | *Lebel* |
| | | | 1NT |
| Pass | 3NT | All Pass | |

West led an inspired ♡J and this was allowed to run to South's king. With little option, Michel Lebel crossed to the ◇Q and finessed in clubs. Fortune favoured the French and when East turned up with Q-x-x in the club suit declarer had five club tricks for a total of ten.

At the other table Shao also opened a 15-17 point 1NT but was raised only to 2NT. With his miserable 4-3-3-3 shape, Shao did not allow his two tens to sway him towards any further move. Once again the ♡J lead was run to South's king. What is the best line in the contract of 2NT?

A losing club finesse would give the defenders at least six tricks (two spades, three hearts and one club). It therefore seemed best to develop a spade trick. He would then score one spade, one heart, four diamonds and two clubs, for a total of eight. This line would succeed whenever hearts broke 4-3, which was a better chance than that of a club finesse. Indeed, the chance of a 4-3 heart break was much better than normal, since if West had five hearts, East would surely have played an honour on the first trick.

Zi Jian Shao duly played on spades and found that West had led from a doubleton heart. He was one down in 2NT when game had been made in the other room. France won the match, a board or two later, by just 196-193. If Shao had followed Lebel's line of play, he would have made 2NT with two overtricks. China would have edged home by a single IMP!

---

Next we will see a deal where one declarer goes down in game at the four level, while another strays to the five level and makes his contract. The deal arose in the 1998 Rosenblum, contested in Lille:

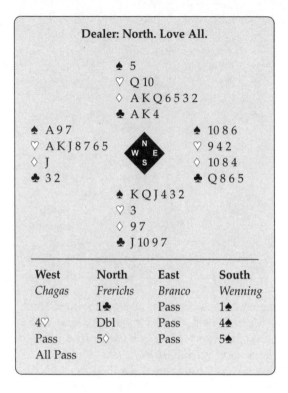

**Dealer: North. Love All.**

|   |   |   |
|---|---|---|
| | ♠ 5 | |
| | ♡ Q 10 | |
| | ◇ A K Q 6 5 3 2 | |
| | ♣ A K 4 | |
| ♠ A 9 7 | | ♠ 10 8 6 |
| ♡ A K J 8 7 6 5 | | ♡ 9 4 2 |
| ◇ J | | ◇ 10 8 4 |
| ♣ 3 2 | | ♣ Q 8 6 5 |
| | ♠ K Q J 4 3 2 | |
| | ♡ 3 | |
| | ◇ 9 7 | |
| | ♣ J 10 9 7 | |

| West | North | East | South |
|------|-------|------|-------|
| *Chagas* | *Frerichs* | *Branco* | *Wenning* |
| | 1♣ | Pass | 1♠ |
| 4♡ | Dbl | Pass | 4♠ |
| Pass | 5◇ | Pass | 5♠ |
| All Pass | | | |

The auction started with a strong club and a natural spade response, Gabriel Chagas entering with the practical overcall of 4♡. North had already expressed lack of interest in spades, with his penalty double of 4♡, and it seems that he should have let matters rest in 4♠. Hans Frerichs decided to correct to 5◇, though, a contract that would be dispatched by two rounds of hearts. (The heart-ruff entry to dummy would then be removed before declarer had set up the spades.) The German South persisted to 5♠ and there matters rested. How would you play this contract when West leads two top hearts and you ruff the second round?

If you simply lead the king of trumps, West will lock you in the dummy and you will run into a trump promotion even when you are lucky enough to find a 3-3 trump break. Ulrich Wenning saw that he needed to remove West's minor-suit cards before playing on trumps – a play known as the 'Dentist's Coup'.

Since he himself held nine diamonds between the hands and only seven clubs, the odds strongly favoured West holding two clubs and only one diamond. Wenning duly cashed the two minor-suit aces, followed by the ♣K. Success so far! West followed all the way. Declarer then played the king of trumps to West's ace. Chagas had only major-suit cards left in his hand. When he returned a third round of hearts, declarer ruffed and drew trumps. He had walked a tightrope, yes, but the contract was made.

This was the bidding at the other table:

| West | North | East | South |
|------|-------|------|-------|
| *Schroeder* | *Villas Boas* | *Marsal* | *Campos* |
| | 1◊ | Pass | 1♠ |
| Dbl | 3◊ | Pass | 3♠ |
| 4♡ | Pass | Pass | 4♠ |
| All Pass | | | |

Dick Schroeder's take-out double, rather than some bid in hearts, is hard to explain. The Brazilians bought the contract one level lower and again two rounds of hearts forced declarer to ruff the second round. Whereas the best line in 5♠ had been clear, it was less apparent how to play 4♠. It was not at all attractive to cash the two top clubs early, for example, because declarer might then lose two trumps, a heart and a club.

Campos decided to lead the ♠K immediately. When West took the ace and exited with the ◊J, won in the dummy, Joao Paulo Campos tried a second top diamond. West ruffed and exited with a club. Since West's double suggested length in both hearts and clubs, he was likely to hold the ♣Q. In any case, declarer had little option but to run the club exit to his hand. East produced the ♣Q and returned a diamond to promote yet another trump trick for the defenders. The Brazilian was two down at the four level, where his adversary had succeeded at the five level.

How about game failing at one table and a slam making at another? Here is one such deal that you may not have seen before. It arose in the 1984 Olympiad, with Panama facing New Zealand:

---

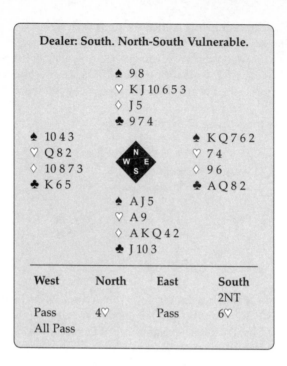

Dealer: South. North-South Vulnerable.

|  | ♠ 9 8 |  |
|  | ♡ K J 10 6 5 3 |  |
|  | ◇ J 5 |  |
|  | ♣ 9 7 4 |  |

| ♠ 10 4 3 |  | ♠ K Q 7 6 2 |
| ♡ Q 8 2 |  | ♡ 7 4 |
| ◇ 10 8 7 3 |  | ◇ 9 6 |
| ♣ K 6 5 |  | ♣ A Q 8 2 |

|  | ♠ A J 5 |  |
|  | ♡ A 9 |  |
|  | ◇ A K Q 4 2 |  |
|  | ♣ J 10 3 |  |

| West | North | East | South |
|------|-------|------|-------|
|      |       |      | 2NT   |
| Pass | 4♡    | Pass | 6♡    |
| All Pass |   |      |       |

Whether or not three-level transfer responses are being used, what is the meaning of a direct leap to game such as North's 4♡ here? There is room for doubt on the matter and the Panama North-South were apparently not in agreement. If North's response was invitational, South felt that he had a fair number of top tricks to add to North's long heart suit. Was it too much to hope for ♡K-Q-x-x-x-x and the ♣K?

North's hand fell short on both of these requirements but all was well when East led a very reasonable (from his point of view) ♠K. Declarer won with the ace, picked up the trumps with a finesse and claimed twelve tricks. "Well bid, partner!"

At the other table the New Zealand North-South failed to realise the slam potential of the hand and stopped in an unambitious game. South was declarer, after a transfer sequence and West led a low club. The defenders quickly pocketed three club tricks, East exiting with the ♠K. For some reason declarer now played for the drop in trumps. He was able to get his spade loser away, yes, but that was still one down. You might make some case for this line in a pairs tournament but at IMPs he should surely have finessed West for the ♡Q, giving himself the best chance of making the game. The result was one down in game when his counterpart had brought home the slam.

On the next deal, from the 1962 Bermuda Bowl, one declarer fails in 5◇ where his opposite number succeeds in 6◇. See what you make of it.

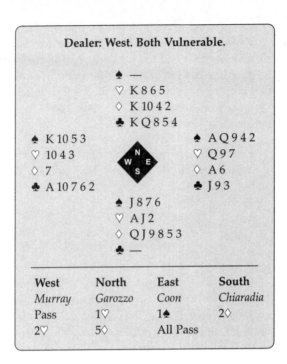

| West | North | East | South |
|------|-------|------|-------|
| *Murray* | *Garozzo* | *Coon* | *Chiaradia* |
| Pass | 1♡ | 1♠ | 2◇ |
| 2♡ | 5◇ | All Pass | |

Eugenio Chiaradia ruffed the spade lead and ran the ♣Q to West's ace, throwing a spade. West played a trump to his partner's ace and discarded a spade on the trump return. Declarer ruffed a club in his hand and returned to dummy with a spade ruff. The ♣K followed by a second club ruff revealed that West still had a stopper in the suit. Rather than simply take a heart finesse through East, which would have won, Chiaradia cashed his last two trumps. This was the end position:

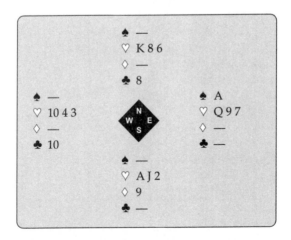

On the last trump West had to discard a heart. The ♣8 was thrown from dummy and East pitched the ♠A. Knowing that West had been squeezed down to two hearts, declarer had to guess who had started with the ♡Q. Recalling West's earlier cue-bid raise of the spade overcall, Chiaradia decided to play him for a 9-count rather than a 7-count. He played to drop the ♡Q and went one down. No-one could be accused of underbidding when the deal was replayed:

| West | North | East | South |
|------|-------|------|-------|
| *Belladonna* | *Nail* | *Avarelli* | *Mathe* |
| Pass | Pass | 1♠ | 2◇ |
| 4♠ | 6◇ | Pass | Pass |
| Dbl | All Pass | | |

Lew Mathe ruffed the spade lead and called for a club honour. When no cover came, he ruffed in his hand and continued to cross-ruff the black suits. All four spades were ruffed in the dummy. He then finessed the ♡J successfully and played the trump queen. On regaining the lead, he drew the last trump and claimed the contract. The slam can be beaten only if West leads a trump, East winning and playing a second trump.

We're nearing the end of the chapter and you are probably expecting to see something fairly racy. How about 3NT failing when 6NT is successful? The deal arose at the 1997 *Macallan* Pairs in London.

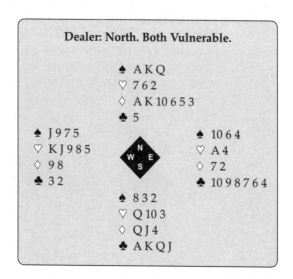

**Dealer: North. Both Vulnerable.**

```
                    ♠ A K Q
                    ♡ 7 6 2
                    ◇ A K 10 6 5 3
                    ♣ 5
  ♠ J 9 7 5                        ♠ 10 6 4
  ♡ K J 9 8 5        N             ♡ A 4
  ◇ 9 8          W       E         ◇ 7 2
  ♣ 3 2              S             ♣ 10 9 8 7 6 4
                    ♠ 8 3 2
                    ♡ Q 10 3
                    ◇ Q J 4
                    ♣ A K Q J
```

| West | North | East | South |
|------|-------|------|-------|
| *Szwarc* | *Lauria* | *Bompis* | *Versace* |
| | 1◊ | Pass | 2♣ |
| Pass | 2◊ | Pass | 2NT |
| Pass | 3◊ | Pass | 3♡ |
| Dbl | 4♣ | Pass | 4NT |
| Pass | 5◊ | Pass | 6NT |
| All Pass | | | |

Lorenzo Lauria and Alfredo Versace are one of the world's strongest pairs. Having paid this tribute, we feel free to say that we do not admire their bidding here. When bids such as 2◊ and 2NT are forcing, as in the two-over-one systems, it can be difficult for either player to express his strength. Auctions tend to ramble on and eventually rely on mere guesswork.

A heart would be an obvious lead against 3NT. Against 6NT it would be a bizarre choice, particularly when the contract had been bid despite West having advertised strength in the suit. Henri Szwarc has our full sympathy for his spade lead. It must have been a sickening moment when declarer spread his hand, claiming all thirteen tricks.

Three North-South pairs (out of eight) bid a slam on this deal and two were successful. The other successful pair was Michael Rosenberg and Simon Deutsch. They made 6◊ from the North seat when Gabriel Chagas elected not to lead the ♡A even though his partner, Zia Mahmood, had made a lead-directing double for hearts during the auction. Why? Well, some boards earlier, Zia had made a psychic lead-directing double on three small, causing declarer to take a losing line. Suspecting Zia of attempting to repeat this triumph, Gabriel Chagas opted for a spade lead! The loss just about cancelled the gain from the previous psych, but it gave reporters a good story.

What happened to the five North-South pairs who showed some restraint and stopped at the game level? No fewer than three of them went down in 3NT, losing five heart tricks. Despite North-South holding 31 points between them, no game is possible against best defence.

We end with a deal where a grand slam succeeded but a small slam in the same denomination failed by four tricks. It happened in a match between Canada and USA, during the 1968 Ladies Olympiad:

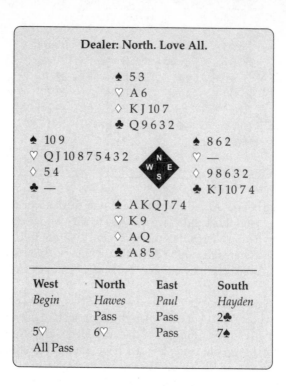

**Dealer: North. Love All.**

```
                    ♠ 5 3
                    ♡ A 6
                    ◇ K J 10 7
                    ♣ Q 9 6 3 2
   ♠ 10 9                        ♠ 8 6 2
   ♡ Q J 10 8 7 5 4 3 2          ♡ —
   ◇ 5 4                         ◇ 9 8 6 3 2
   ♣ —                           ♣ K J 10 7 4
                    ♠ A K Q J 7 4
                    ♡ K 9
                    ◇ A Q
                    ♣ A 8 5
```

| West | North | East | South |
|------|-------|------|-------|
| *Begin* | *Hawes* | *Paul* | *Hayden* |
|  | Pass | Pass | 2♣ |
| 5♡ | 6♡ | Pass | 7♠ |
| All Pass | | | |

West fondly imagined that her 5♡ overcall would make it difficult to bid a slam. Who was she kidding? Two bids later her opponents were installed in a grand slam. The best contract is 7NT, to avoid the danger of a ruff, but from Dorothy Hayden's viewpoint it was very likely that her partner's 6♡ bid had been made on a void rather than the ace. When West led a diamond against 7♠, declarer drew trumps and claimed the contract.

Should East have made a Lightner double of 7♠? It is generally accepted that Lightner cannot ask for a lead of partner's suit. As we see it, East should have doubled 6♡ to suggest a heart lead. It's not a 100% action, since the final contract might be 6NT, but it looks best. Having said that, West's decision to lead a diamond was an odd one. Since partner could not make a Lightner double if she held a heart void, why not lead the nine-card suit and hope partner can ruff? This was the other auction:

| West | North | East | South |
|------|-------|------|-------|
| Baron | O'Brien | Walsh | Mark |
| | Pass | Pass | 2♣ |
| 6♡ | Pass | Pass | 6♠ |
| All Pass | | | |

West followed her brave pre-empt with a fine lead – the ♡2. East ruffed and returned a club, declarer rising with the ace. West ruffed this trick and the defenders ended with four trump tricks and the ♣K.

# 18
# Did You Mean to Throw That Ace Away?

It is not particularly rare for a defender to throw away an ace. The two most common reasons are to avoid being thrown in and to create an entry to partner's hand. Disdaining such ordinary fare, we will present you with a rarer spectacle in this chapter – declarers tossing away aces with wanton abandon.

The first deal comes from a match between France and Slovenia in the 1993 European Championship:

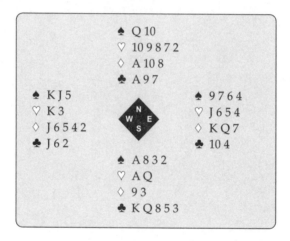

Michel Lebel played in 3NT on the South cards and a fourth-best ◇4 was led. The Slovenian East won with the queen but, uncertain who held the ◇J, did not continue the suit. He switched to the ♡4, drawing the queen and king, and West returned the ◇2 to East's king. This time East did clear the diamond suit, returning the ◇7. Suppose you had been the declarer. How would you have played the contract from this point?

You must assume that the clubs are good for five tricks, which brings your total to eight. One chance of a ninth trick is to lead a spade to the ten. If this forces East's king, the safe hand will be on lead and dummy's ♠Q will be good for the extra trick you need. Lebel spotted a better line. On the third round of diamonds he discarded the ♡A! The two red aces made a pretty sight on the baize and, more importantly, the way was now clear to lead dummy's ♡10. East won with the jack, which was always likely after his previous lead of the ♡4, and declarer now had nine tricks. He had thrown away one winner (the ♡A) and scored two winners (the ♡9 and ♡8) in exchange.

Stig Werdelin of Sweden is our next declarer, competing in the 2003 European Open Championships in Menton:

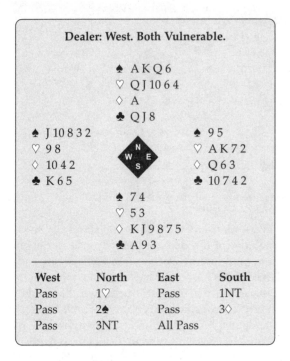

Dealer: West. Both Vulnerable.

|  | ♠ AKQ6 |  |
|---|---|---|
|  | ♡ QJ1064 |  |
|  | ◇ A |  |
|  | ♣ QJ8 |  |
| ♠ J10832 |  | ♠ 95 |
| ♡ 98 |  | ♡ AK72 |
| ◇ 1042 |  | ◇ Q63 |
| ♣ K65 |  | ♣ 10742 |
|  | ♠ 74 |  |
|  | ♡ 53 |  |
|  | ◇ KJ9875 |  |
|  | ♣ A93 |  |

| West | North | East | South |
|---|---|---|---|
| Pass | 1♡ | Pass | 1NT |
| Pass | 2♠ | Pass | 3◇ |
| Pass | 3NT | All Pass | |

Werdelin won the ♠2 lead in dummy and played the ♡Q, which was allowed to hold. East captured the ♡J and returned the ♠9 to the dummy. Declarer tried his luck with another heart but West discarded a diamond. East won the third round of hearts with the seven and switched to a club, won by West's king. The club return was won with dummy's jack and declarer cashed the ◇A to leave this position:

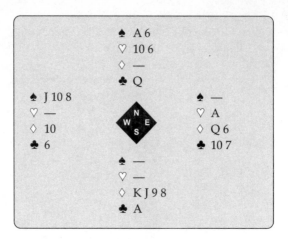

Declarer has already lost two hearts and a club. How should he continue?

If the ◇Q was now bare, Werdelin could simply cross to the ♣A and score the remainder of the diamond suit. If instead East held ◇Q-x, a throw-in would be required. Declarer marked time by cashing the ♠A and East released the ♣7. Declarer had a count on the majors and it now seemed almost certain that East still held two diamonds. On the ♠A declarer promptly jettisoned the ♣A from his hand! He was then able to cash the ♣Q, remaining in dummy, and end-play East with a heart to win the last two diamond tricks in his hand. Brilliant play, indeed.

We have seen a black ace discarded on a black ace, and a red ace discarded on a red ace. It's time for a black ace on a black king and our venue is the 2003 Superliga in Poland:

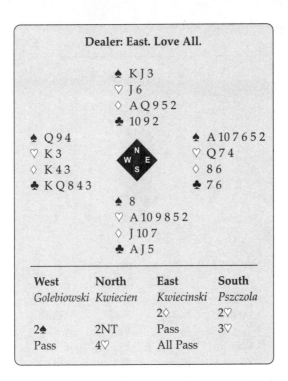

Dealer: East. Love All.

|  |  |
|---|---|
| | ♠ K J 3 |
| | ♡ J 6 |
| | ◇ A Q 9 5 2 |
| | ♣ 10 9 2 |

| | |
|---|---|
| ♠ Q 9 4 | ♠ A 10 7 6 5 2 |
| ♡ K 3 | ♡ Q 7 4 |
| ◇ K 4 3 | ◇ 8 6 |
| ♣ K Q 8 4 3 | ♣ 7 6 |

|  |
|---|
| ♠ 8 |
| ♡ A 10 9 8 5 2 |
| ◇ J 10 7 |
| ♣ A J 5 |

| West | North | East | South |
|---|---|---|---|
| Golebiowski | Kwiecien | Kwiecinski | Pszczola |
| | | 2◇ | 2♡ |
| 2♠ | 2NT | Pass | 3♡ |
| Pass | 4♡ | All Pass | |

East opened with a Multi 2◇ and if you think the North-South bidding looks somewhat unconvincing we agree with you! The play, however, was great. West led the ♠9 and Jacek Pszczola inserted dummy's jack, forcing the ace. How would you continue when East returns the ♣7?

Pszczola played cleverly by inserting the ♣J, won by West's queen. He could then win the low club continuation in the dummy. A club ruff was threatened but declarer avoided this by discarding his ♣A on the ♠K! He then took a losing trump finesse, won the diamond switch with the queen and finessed again in trumps for the contract.

Do you see why it was necessary to play the ♣J on the first round? Suppose declarer plays low, West winning and returning the suit. Declarer has to win in the South hand and cross to dummy with a diamond. He discards the ♣A on the ♠K, as before, and runs the jack of trumps to West's king. Now West plays the ♣K and East throws his last diamond! There is no entry to dummy to repeat the trump finesse.

The only opening lead to beat the contract is a club honour. Declarer cannot then avoid two black-suit losers and two further losers in the trump suit.

It's near the end of the chapter, so we will up the tempo and show you a deal where declarer threw away not only an ace but also a king.

---

The heroine in the South seat was Barbara Tepper from New York:

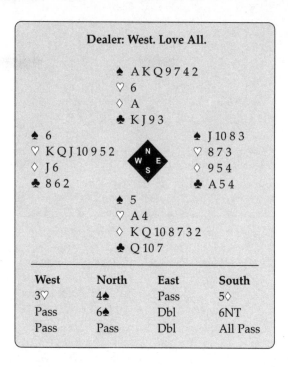

**Dealer: West. Love All.**

```
                    ♠ A K Q 9 7 4 2
                    ♡ 6
                    ◇ A
                    ♣ K J 9 3
♠ 6                                    ♠ J 10 8 3
♡ K Q J 10 9 5 2                       ♡ 8 7 3
◇ J 6                                  ◇ 9 5 4
♣ 8 6 2                                ♣ A 5 4
                    ♠ 5
                    ♡ A 4
                    ◇ K Q 10 8 7 3 2
                    ♣ Q 10 7
```

| West | North | East | South |
|------|-------|------|-------|
| 3♡ | 4♠ | Pass | 5◇ |
| Pass | 6♠ | Dbl | 6NT |
| Pass | Pass | Dbl | All Pass |

We are about to admire Barbara's card-play but we will withhold such praise from the bidding! As we see it, South had no reason to bid over 4♠ and certainly could not expect 5◇ to be a better contract than 4♠. Whatever South's forward move meant, it was reasonable for North to place the ♣A in partner's hand and attempt a slam.

East's double of 6♠ might well have found its way into our Chapter 20 on disastrous doubles! He could expect 6♠ to go one down, yes, but was it worth doubling in the hope of converting +50 into +100? If South held a massive diamond suit there might easily be no defence to 6NT. As players do, he felt obliged to double South's rescue into no-trumps.

West led the ♡K and Barbara Tepper ducked! It was surely obvious that declarer held the ♡A, otherwise she would have bid 6NT with a heart stopper that was at best eight-high. Nevertheless, West continued woodenly with the ♡Q. This was what Barbara had been hoping for. She discarded dummy's blocking ◇A and played the ◇K and ◇Q. Yes! The ◇J fell doubleton. Did that give her twelve tricks? No, only eleven, so there was further work to do.

Declarer ran the diamond suit and on the last round threw dummy's ♣K, retaining ♠A-K-Q-9 in the dummy. East was squeezed in the black suits. He threw the ♣A, in the desperate hope that his partner held the

♣Q, and declarer scored one club and three spades for her contract.

We will end with a curiosity, where declarer discards an ace in order to promote an eight into an entry. The deal was played in Bydgoszcz, Poland, in 2001, and the declarer was Norway's Jon Lokeborg:

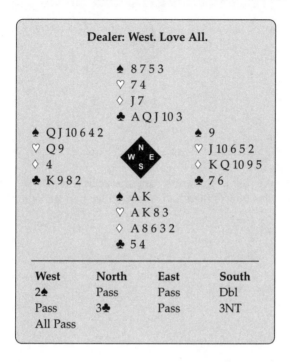

Dealer: West. Love All.

|  | ♠ 8 7 5 3 |  |
|  | ♡ 7 4 |  |
|  | ◊ J 7 |  |
|  | ♣ A Q J 10 3 |  |

| ♠ Q J 10 6 4 2 | | ♠ 9 |
| ♡ Q 9 | | ♡ J 10 6 5 2 |
| ◊ 4 | | ◊ K Q 10 9 5 |
| ♣ K 9 8 2 | | ♣ 7 6 |

|  | ♠ A K |  |
|  | ♡ A K 8 3 |  |
|  | ◊ A 8 6 3 2 |  |
|  | ♣ 5 4 |  |

| West | North | East | South |
|------|-------|------|-------|
| 2♠ | Pass | Pass | Dbl |
| Pass | 3♣ | Pass | 3NT |
| All Pass | | | |

North-South were playing Lebensohl in this situation, so the 3♣ bid promised some values (with a weak hand, North would have bid 2NT instead). West led the ♣Q, picking up his partner's ♣9, and Lokeborg won with the king. How would you play the contract?

Declarer continued with a winning club finesse. It was possible that East had held up, holding the ♣K. Since the position would be hopeless in that case, Lokeborg assumed that West held the ♣K. If he had started with only two or three clubs, dummy's suit would be good and the contract a formality. What if West held four clubs? Declarer could see a way home if West's shape was 6-2-1-4. He cashed his winners in the red suits, which did indeed remove West's holdings there, and took another club finesse. The next trick brought bad news. When the ♣A was played, East showed out. Would you have seen how to recover?

These cards remained:

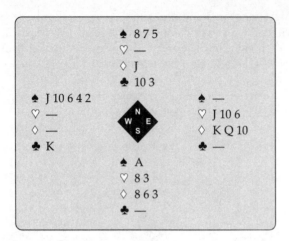

Lokeborg led a club from dummy and discarded the ♠A! West could cash two top spades but he then had to surrender two tricks to the dummy.

# 19
# An Imaginative Escape

The 1995 European Championships were contested in Portugal's Vilamoura. In the match between Italy and Israel, Alfredo Versace was faced with a very awkward bidding problem. Take the North cards here and see how would you have approached it.

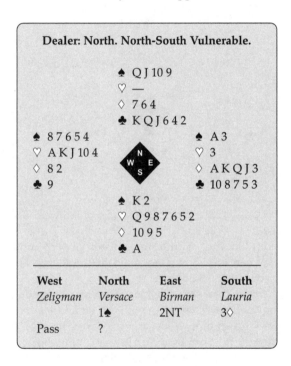

**Dealer: North. North-South Vulnerable.**

|  | ♠ Q J 10 9 |  |
|---|---|---|
|  | ♡ — |  |
|  | ♢ 7 6 4 |  |
|  | ♣ K Q J 6 4 2 |  |
| ♠ 8 7 6 5 4 |  | ♠ A 3 |
| ♡ A K J 10 4 |  | ♡ 3 |
| ♢ 8 2 |  | ♢ A K Q J 3 |
| ♣ 9 |  | ♣ 10 8 7 5 3 |
|  | ♠ K 2 |  |
|  | ♡ Q 9 8 7 6 5 2 |  |
|  | ♢ 10 9 5 |  |
|  | ♣ A |  |

| West | North | East | South |
|---|---|---|---|
| Zeligman | Versace | Birman | Lauria |
|  | 1♠ | 2NT | 3♢ |
| Pass | ? |  |  |

You open 1♠ and . . . What, you wouldn't have opened 1♠? You're playing canapé openings, where the first bid can be made in the second-best suit. You still wouldn't have opened 1♠? Well, just accept it then and see what happens. East overcalls with the Unusual No-trump, showing length in both minors and your partner bids 3♢. In the method known as 'Unusual *vs* Unusual', this shows length in hearts and game-try values. West passes, with an ominous lack of interest in proceedings, and it is your bid. What do you say?

An excellent idea as it had seemed at the time, Versace was beginning to regret his 1♠ opening. Hearts were surely stacked over his partner and he could hardly rebid a spade suit of just four cards. As for clubs, they were known to be stacked in the East hand. Versace decided

---

to pass the artificial 3◊ bid! David Birman concluded that his opponent had suffered an aberration and passed happily.

When West led the ♣9, Lorenzo Lauria won with the ace and ruffed a heart. A spade was played and Birman rose with the ace, declarer unblocking the king. If East drew trumps at this stage, he would have to present a bushel of tricks to the dummy. He therefore played a second club. Lauria ruffed with the ◊10, played a spade to dummy and ruffed a third round of clubs with the ◊9. These cards remained:

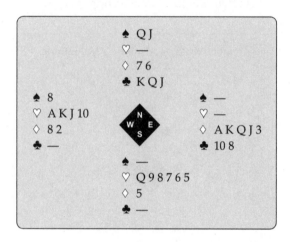

Lauria exited with the ◊5 and the bulletin report continues: "The defenders now had to play well to avoid presenting declarer with two more tricks rather than just one."

In fact there are two ways in which the defenders could have scored the remaining tricks. West can rise with the ◊8 and lead a top heart. If declarer ruffs with dummy's last trump, East will overruff and give partner a club ruff. West can then cash his remaining top heart, on which East throws his last club. The play is similar if declarer ruffs the second heart instead of the first. Alternatively, West can play low on the ◊5 exit. East wins with the jack and plays a low trump to West's eight, allowing West to cash two hearts.

Be that as it may, Lauria scored a fine six tricks to go only 300 down. At the other table his Israeli counterpart went 500 down in 3♣ doubled, giving the Italians a 5-IMP swing.

If West had found the best lead of a trump, the defenders could have taken five trumps, one spade and three hearts, matching the 500 penalty at the other table. Still, let us salute the imagination of Versace in passing the artificial bid of 3◊. Had he taken any other action he would surely have lost IMPs instead of gaining them.

# 20
# Axe or Boomerang?

In this chapter we will look at some doubles that seemed a good idea at the time but, in practice, turned out to be a spectacularly bad idea. Sometimes they tipped off declarer as to the lie of the cards, sometimes they persuaded the opponents to run elsewhere.

We begin at the 2000 Bermuda Bowl final, with Brazil facing USA. Roberto Mello's dazzling play on the following deal would not have been possible without a tell-tale double.

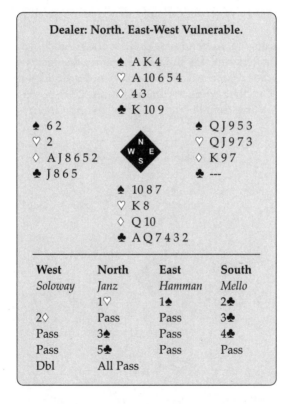

**Dealer: North. East-West Vulnerable.**

|  | ♠ A K 4 |  |
|---|---|---|
|  | ♡ A 10 6 5 4 |  |
|  | ◇ 4 3 |  |
|  | ♣ K 10 9 |  |
| ♠ 6 2 |  | ♠ Q J 9 5 3 |
| ♡ 2 |  | ♡ Q J 9 7 3 |
| ◇ A J 8 6 5 2 |  | ◇ K 9 7 |
| ♣ J 8 6 5 |  | ♣ --- |
|  | ♠ 10 8 7 |  |
|  | ♡ K 8 |  |
|  | ◇ Q 10 |  |
|  | ♣ A Q 7 4 3 2 |  |

| West | North | East | South |
|---|---|---|---|
| *Soloway* | *Janz* | *Hamman* | *Mello* |
|  | 1♡ | 1♠ | 2♣ |
| 2◇ | Pass | Pass | 3♣ |
| Pass | 3♠ | Pass | 4♣ |
| Pass | 5♣ | Pass | Pass |
| Dbl | All Pass |  |  |

North's 3♠ showed a spade stopper and asked South to bid no-trumps if he could stop the other enemy suit, diamonds. South's ◇Q-10 were not up to the task and the bidding proceeded towards the club game. At the other table, a similar auction led to 5♣ undoubled. Without the warning, Eric Rodwell played a low trump to the king and finished two off.

Here, Paul Soloway doubled 5♣ and led his singleton heart. Declarer

---

won East's ♡9 with the king and, aided by the double, played a club to the nine! Hamman discarded a spade but the play was far from over. Mello drew all of Soloway's trumps, at the same time subjecting poor Bob Hamman (who was down to ♠Q-J-9 ♡Q-J-7-3 ◇K-9) to unbearable pressure. Since a spade discard was out of the question and a heart discard would allow Mello to establish a long card in the suit, Hamman discarded the ◇9.

Mello exited with a low diamond to East's bare king and Hamman returned the ♠Q, won in the dummy. When Mello continued with a low heart, Hamman had to win with the jack and concede a trick on his return. South's remaining diamond loser could then be discarded.

What would have happened if Hamman had unblocked his ◇K on the fourth trump? Mello had the answer: "I cash my top spades and exit with a diamond to West. He can only play diamonds, and then East is squeezed." It was 12 IMPs to Brazil.

We move now to a second type of disastrous double. The opponents arrive in a hopeless contract and you announce this fact with a double. Taking heed, the opponents try their luck elsewhere and end up making the contract. Our first example comes from the 2003 European Open in Menton, with teams from Poland and Israel in opposition:

---

**Dealer: South. Love All.**

```
                    ♠ 10 9 8 7 5 3 2
                    ♡ 5 3
                    ◇ 10 8
                    ♣ 6 4
♠ —                                    ♠ A K Q 6 4
♡ 10 8 7 4          N                  ♡ 9 2
◇ J 7 3 2       W       E              ◇ 6 5 4
♣ A J 9 8 2         S                  ♣ 7 5 3
                    ♠ J
                    ♡ A K Q J 6
                    ◇ A K Q 9
                    ♣ K Q 10
```

| West | North | East | South |
|------|-------|------|-------|
|      | *Schneider* |  | *Barel* |
|      |       |      | 2♣ |
| Pass | 2♠ | Pass | 3NT |
| Pass | 4♠ | Dbl | 4NT |
| Pass | Pass | Dbl | All Pass |

---

Strange as it may seem, North's first response of 2♠ was reported as non-forcing. South rebid 3NT, an easy make, but North corrected to the spade game. Would you have doubled on those East cards?

The best way to express delight at such a final contract is to pass. South has announced a huge hand, short in spades, and East has hardly any defence to a non-spade suit contract. Unable to restrain himself, East doubled 'the only contract he could beat'. Michael Barel was quick to run to 4NT and, in the way that players do, East also doubled this contract.

With no spade to lead, West tried his luck with the ♡8. Declarer won, ran five rounds of hearts and then played the ♣Q. If West won, he would have to return one of the minors, surrendering a tenth trick. Sensing this, he allowed the ♣Q to win. Barel was not to be denied. He played three top diamonds and threw West on lead with a fourth round of diamonds. With only clubs in his hand, West had to give declarer a second club trick and the contract of 4NT doubled was made, for a score of +610. At the other table, the Israelis wisely let 4♠ go peacefully two down, undoubled, collecting 12 IMPs as a reward.

The next deal is extraordinary because small slams in two different suits were doubled, with the result that the doubled side moved to a different suit. India faced Iceland in the 1992 Olympiad:

---

**Dealer: South. North-South Vulnerable.**

|  |  |  |
|---|---|---|
|  | ♠ A 10 8 |  |
|  | ♡ A K 7 |  |
|  | ◇ 4 |  |
|  | ♣ A K J 7 6 5 |  |
| ♠ 6 4 3 |  | ♠ K J 5 |
| ♡ 8 5 |  | ♡ 10 |
| ◇ A K J 8 3 |  | ◇ Q 10 7 6 5 |
| ♣ 8 4 3 |  | ♣ Q 10 9 2 |
|  | ♠ Q 9 7 2 |  |
|  | ♡ Q J 9 6 4 3 2 |  |
|  | ◇ 9 2 |  |
|  | ♣ — |  |

| West | North | East | South |
|------|-------|------|-------|
| Gupta | Sverrisson | Shah | Baldursson |
|  |  |  | 2♣ |
| 2◇ | Dbl | 4◇ | 4♡ |
| Pass | 6♡ | Dbl | Pass |
| Pass | 6♠ | All Pass |  |

---

Can you guess what South's 2♣ opening meant? You certainly wouldn't be helped in your guess by looking at the cards that South actually held. The opening showed one of three hand types: a weak two in diamonds, a weak two-suiter with both majors or a very strong balanced hand. You don't regard that as a two-suiter in the majors? No indeed, but players who use these obstructive openings tend to stretch them to the limits or even, as here, well beyond the limits.

Sigurdur Sverrisson's double asked partner to identify his hand-type. Jon Baldursson made a free 4♡ bid, no doubt hoping to indicate that he had longer hearts than spades (a pass would have indicated a weak major two-suiter.) It seemed that no damage had been done when North raised to 6♡. That is the par contract and can easily be made by setting up the clubs. The Indian East found some reason to double this contract, however, and North then paused to reconsider the situation. Perhaps the hearts were breaking poorly and the hand would play better in spades? North 'corrected' the contract to 6♠, which was strangely passed out and went three down. At the other table the Indian South opened a weak 2♡ on his cards and was soon entering +1430 on his score-card for a gain of 17 IMPs.

Adventures enough on one hand, you may think, but the same deal produced an equally spectacular auction in a different match:

| West | North | East | South |
|------|-------|------|-------|
| *Versace* | *Tuszynski* | *Lauria* | *Kowalski* |
| | | | Pass |
| Pass | 1♣ | 1◊ | 1♡ |
| 4◊ | 6♣ | Dbl | Pass |
| Pass | 6♡ | Dbl | All Pass |

The Poles were heading for an inglorious 6♣ when Lorenzo Lauria expressed his views about this contract. It did not prove to be a sage move, for North swiftly corrected to the cold contract of 6♡. Plus 1660 meant 14 IMPs for Poland when Giorgio Duboin declined to open on the South cards at the other table and the Italian North-South let the bidding die in 4♡.

It had been an amazing deal. At one table East doubled a cold slam and drove the opponents into a failing slam. At another, East doubled a failing slam and drove the opponents into a making slam.

On the deal we have just seen, the opponents moved simply from one denomination to another. What if they also move a level higher? Perhaps they are doubled in a small slam and rescue themselves into a grand slam in a different suit? Such a situation is not so rare as you may think. The first, almost unbelievable, example arose in the 1999 *Cap Gemini* tournament:

Alain Levy had only to pass 6NT and he could have pocketed +200 for four down, assuming the club suit did not become blocked. As the French proverb has it, he decided to add marmalade to the honey by doubling. Tony Forrester had the presence of mind to run to 7♠, a contract that had the immense advantage of being played by South. The spotlight turned on Paul Chemla: would he find the club lead? What would you have led from the West hand?

If East held two top winners in spades or diamonds, a lead of the ♡K would be good enough since Chemla also had the clubs guarded. If East held two top clubs, declarer might well be able to run for home with a string of winners in spades and diamonds. It was difficult to imagine that North-South had attempted 6NT with clubs that were at best ten-high and Chemla eventually led the ♡K. A grateful declarer scored thirteen tricks.

Alain Levy did not receive good odds for his double. Assume that North-South do not run and that West unblocks the ♣Q and ♣J, allowing the contract to go four down doubled. For scoring +800 against a datum of -660, Levy would pick up 16 IMPs. Yes, but without the double he would score 13 IMPs anyway. He ended up losing 13 IMPs, so he was gambling 26 IMPs to pick up an extra 3.

---

At another table, Doris Fischer and Terri Weigkricht reached 6♠ by South. Westerhof doubled as East, and North, fearing that the double was Lightner for a diamond void, ran to 6NT. However, South had made an earlier bid of 4NT and therefore became the declarer in 6NT doubled. When West led the ♡K, the Austrian women scored +1330.

We have no fewer than three more deals in our records where a player doubled 6NT with an ace-king and subsequently conceded a grand slam! Let's treat ourselves to one more example, from the 2001 Las Vegas NABC.

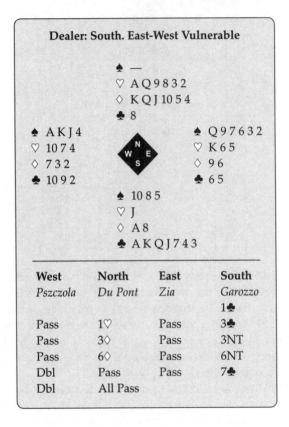

**Dealer: South. East-West Vulnerable**

|  |  |  |  |
|---|---|---|---|
| | ♠ — | | |
| | ♡ A Q 9 8 3 2 | | |
| | ◇ K Q J 10 5 4 | | |
| | ♣ 8 | | |

| ♠ A K J 4 | | ♠ Q 9 7 6 3 2 |
|---|---|---|
| ♡ 10 7 4 | | ♡ K 6 5 |
| ◇ 7 3 2 | | ◇ 9 6 |
| ♣ 10 9 2 | | ♣ 6 5 |

|  |  |  |  |
|---|---|---|---|
| | ♠ 10 8 5 | | |
| | ♡ J | | |
| | ◇ A 8 | | |
| | ♣ A K Q J 7 4 3 | | |

| West | North | East | South |
|---|---|---|---|
| *Pszczola* | *Du Pont* | *Zia* | *Garozzo* |
| | | | 1♣ |
| Pass | 1♡ | Pass | 3♣ |
| Pass | 3◇ | Pass | 3NT |
| Pass | 6◇ | Pass | 6NT |
| Dbl | Pass | Pass | 7♣ |
| Dbl | All Pass | | |

It is always tempting for the superior dummy player in a partnership to 'hog' the contract. Even so, Benito Garozzo may have set some sort of world record for this activity when he stole partner's diamond slam to play in 6NT with a ten-high stopper in the unbid suit. Partner had advertised a massive two-suiter in the reds and there was every chance that her spade control might be by shortage.

Would you have resisted temptation on those West cards? Jacek Pszczola may have struggled with his conscience for a moment but . . . his fingers moved irrevocably towards the red double card. It was not difficult for Garozzo to read the situation. If only to reduce his loss on the deal, he corrected to 7♣, doubled on his left. Dummy came to the rescue with a spade void and the doubled grand was made. Once again the defender had converted a massive plus swing into an equally vast swing in the other direction. A lesson to us all.

Another way that a technically sound double may backfire was discovered by the Greek team in the 2002 European Championships, contested in Salsomaggiore. They faced Ireland on this deal:

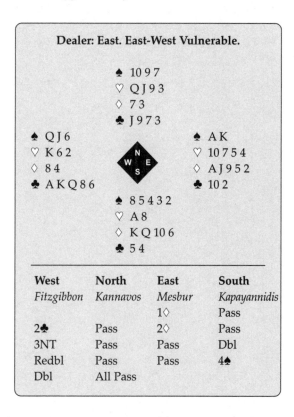

Dealer: East. East-West Vulnerable.

|  | North | | |
|---|---|---|---|
| | ♠ 10 9 7 | | |
| | ♡ Q J 9 3 | | |
| | ◇ 7 3 | | |
| | ♣ J 9 7 3 | | |

| West | | East |
|---|---|---|
| ♠ Q J 6 | | ♠ A K |
| ♡ K 6 2 | | ♡ 10 7 5 4 |
| ◇ 8 4 | | ◇ A J 9 5 2 |
| ♣ A K Q 8 6 | | ♣ 10 2 |

| | South | |
|---|---|---|
| | ♠ 8 5 4 3 2 | |
| | ♡ A 8 | |
| | ◇ K Q 10 6 | |
| | ♣ 5 4 | |

| West | North | East | South |
|---|---|---|---|
| *Fitzgibbon* | *Kannavos* | *Mesbur* | *Kapayannidis* |
| | | 1◇ | Pass |
| 2♣ | Pass | 2◇ | Pass |
| 3NT | Pass | Pass | Dbl |
| Redbl | Pass | Pass | 4♠ |
| Dbl | All Pass | | |

What is the meaning of an 'out-of-the blue' double of 3NT? By convention, it is lead-directing. If no suit has been mentioned, in an auction such as 1NT – 3NT, there are two popular schemes. One is to request specifically a spade lead. The other asks partner to lead the weakest suit in his hand, aiming to hit a strong suit held by the doubler. When suits have been bid, the situation is different. A double suggests strength in dummy's main suit.

Here South was strong in dummy's diamond suit. If West had bid 2NT at his second turn, raised to 3NT, the double would have been a good bet because both opponents would have been limited. It was much more of a gamble here, because West might well have values to spare for his 3NT bid. That was indeed the case and Nick Fitzgibbon was happy to redouble.

As it happens, a diamond lead does beat 3NT and is the only lead to do so. Unfortunately, Kostas Kapayannidis got cold feet when West redoubled and ran to his five-card spade suit. The defenders led a trump against 4♠ doubled and managed to prevent any diamond ruffs, picking up 1100.

In the other room Photis Skoularikis played 3NT from the West seat and made an made the game easily after a heart lead. Greece lost 10 IMPs when they would have gained 14 had Kapayannidis stood the redouble and beaten 3NT.

# 21
# Jaggy's Brilliant Underruff

The 1988 *Cino del Duca* Gold Cup was held in the glittering Palais de Chaillot and the deal below was worthy of the splendid surroundings. Put yourself in the East seat, holding the same cards as Indian maestro, Jaggy Shivdasani, and see what you make of it:

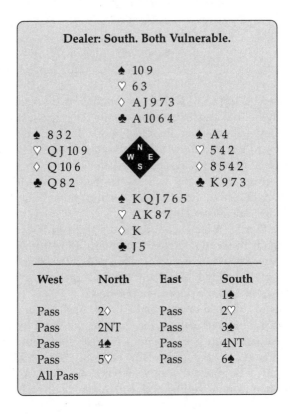

**Dealer: South. Both Vulnerable.**

|  | ♠ 10 9 |  |  |
|---|---|---|---|
|  | ♡ 6 3 |  |  |
|  | ◇ A J 9 7 3 |  |  |
|  | ♣ A 10 6 4 |  |  |

| ♠ 8 3 2 | | ♠ A 4 |
| ♡ Q J 10 9 | | ♡ 5 4 2 |
| ◇ Q 10 6 | | ◇ 8 5 4 2 |
| ♣ Q 8 2 | | ♣ K 9 7 3 |

|  | ♠ K Q J 7 6 5 |
|  | ♡ A K 8 7 |
|  | ◇ K |
|  | ♣ J 5 |

| West | North | East | South |
|------|-------|------|-------|
|      |       |      | 1♠    |
| Pass | 2◇    | Pass | 2♡    |
| Pass | 2NT   | Pass | 3♠    |
| Pass | 4♠    | Pass | 4NT   |
| Pass | 5♡    | Pass | 6♠    |
| All Pass | | | |

A trump lead would have been lethal but some cruel deity had given West a solid heart sequence. The ♡Q duly appeared on the table and declarer was in with a chance. He won with the ♡A and cashed the ◇K. A club to the ace was followed by the ◇A for a club discard. Declarer now had to manoeuvre two heart ruffs and draw the opponents' trumps.

A heart to the king was followed by the first heart ruff. A club ruff returned the lead to the South hand, leaving these cards still to be played:

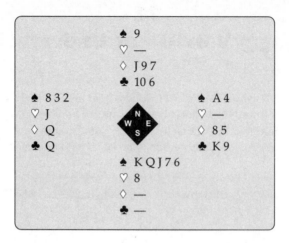

```
                    ♠ 9
                    ♡ —
                    ◇ J 9 7
                    ♣ 10 6
    ♠ 8 3 2                        ♠ A 4
    ♡ J              N             ♡ —
    ◇ Q          W       E        ◇ 8 5
    ♣ Q              S             ♣ K 9
                    ♠ K Q J 7 6
                    ♡ 8
                    ◇ —
                    ♣ —
```

Declarer ruffed his last heart with the ♠9 and it was Jaggy Shivdasani to play a card in the East seat. What would your choice have been?

Overruffing with the ace does not work. Declarer can ruff your minor suit return low and draw trumps. Suppose you throw a diamond instead. With a trump promotion in diamonds no longer a threat, declarer can cross to his hand with a diamond ruff and lead the ♠K. Twelve tricks will result. Since the minor-suit position is symmetrical, a club discard will not succeed either.

Realising that he might need his second card in both the minors, Shivdasani made the brilliant defence of underruffing dummy's ♠9 with the ♠4! Declarer crossed to his hand with a club ruff and led the king of trumps to East's ace. Shivdasani then played his precious second club to promote West's ♠8 and the slam went one down.

Why should this deal bring a smile to our lips? Because if declarer had read East's mind and realised the situation, he could have played a low trump to East's bare ace. His remaining ♠K-Q-J would then have been proof against any promotion. How amusing that would have been for Shivdasani if he had happened to underruff from A-4-3 and his partner had then won the setting trick with a doubleton eight of trumps!

# 22
# Its Own Reward

Performing a brilliant play is satisfying in its own right, but as the perpetrator returns his cards to the wallet he is also hoping that he will net a big swing for his team. In this chapter we will see some truly great plays that netted not a single IMP. In some cases there was a large adverse swing. In such a case virtue must be its own reward.

You are doubled into game and make the contract with a brilliant line of play. Surely you can expect some IMPs in the plus column? Not necessarily. Our first deal occurred in the 1980 Olympiad, with Denmark facing the Philippines:

---

**Dealer: East. East-West Vulnerable.**

```
                    ♠ J 4
                    ♡ 9 7 5
                    ◇ K J 9 5 2
                    ♣ 9 8 4
        ♠ 6 5                      ♠ A Q 9 3 2
        ♡ A Q 6 3       N          ♡ 2
        ◇ Q 8 6 3    W     E       ◇ A 10 7
        ♣ J 10 2        S          ♣ K 7 6 5
                    ♠ K 10 8 7
                    ♡ K J 10 8 4
                    ◇ 4
                    ♣ A Q 3
```

| West | North | East | South |
|------|-------|------|-------|
| *Quiogue* | *J. Norris* | *Tan* | *G. Norris* |
|      |       | 1♠   | 2♡    |
| Pass | Pass  | Dbl  | All Pass |

---

West led the ♠6 to his partner's ace and East defended accurately with a trump return, allowing his partner to play three rounds of the suit. Georg Norris unblocked a high trump from his hand, so that he could win the third round with dummy's ♡9. The ♠J was covered by the queen and king but declarer still seemed to be two tricks short of his target. Hoping to put East under pressure, Norris played off his remaining trumps. This position arose:

---

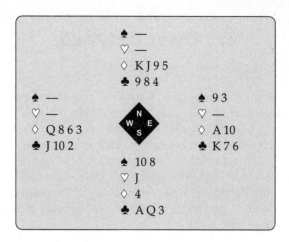

Declarer threw a diamond from dummy on the last trump. What could poor East throw? If he released a spade, declarer would cash two spade winners and then end-play East for the second extra trick. East actually chose to throw a club, but ace and another club set up South's queen. On lead with the ♣K, East cashed the ◊A and led a spade, declarer finessing the ♠8 for the contract.

An interesting position would arise if East bares his ◊A. He would then be thrown on lead with a diamond, leaving these cards out:

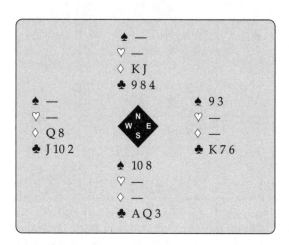

East would doubtless exit with a club now, but declarer finesses the ♣Q and cashes the ♣A. It makes no difference whether East unblocks the ♣K under the ace. One or other defender will have to win the third club and then concede two tricks to either the spade or diamond tenace.

Did Norris gain a handsome swing for this dazzling performance?

No, just another flat board. At the other table the contract was once again 2♡ doubled but, after a spade lead to the ace, East switched to a club. The Philippines declarer could ruff his spade losers and was therefore spared the need for brilliancy.

Let's see now an excellent defence that brought no reward on the scoresheet. We travel back in time to the 1958 European Championship, with Italy facing Great Britain:

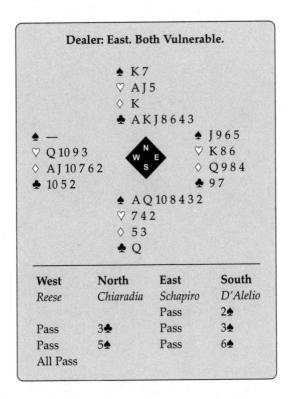

**Dealer: East. Both Vulnerable.**

| West | North | East | South |
|------|-------|------|-------|
| *Reese* | *Chiaradia* | *Schapiro* | *D'Alelio* |
| | | Pass | 2♠ |
| Pass | 3♣ | Pass | 3♠ |
| Pass | 5♠ | Pass | 6♠ |
| All Pass | | | |

Massimo D'Alelio's 2♠ opening was not a weak-two opening as we know it today. It showed a good suit and a maximum of around 12 points. Eugenio Chiaradia's subsequent 5♠ asked partner to bid a small slam if his trumps were strong. It was a fine piece of bidding by the Italians. However, Terence Reese found the only winning defence of ace and another diamond, forcing the dummy to ruff, and the 4-0 trump break then spelt defeat. Surely, with such a combination of sharp defence and good luck, East-West could expect a swing in their direction?

At the other table both South and West declined to open on their hands. (How many would pass nowadays?) Alan Truscott (North) opened 3NT, which was meant to show a solid minor and a potential guard in the other suits. Maurice Harrison Gray passed on the South cards, when many would prefer to bid the spade game. All would have been well if East had chosen to lead a spade. No, he led a diamond and the Italians took the first six tricks for two down vulnerable. Great Britain therefore lost 2 IMPs on the board.

Terence Reese was a world master at the art of sarcasm. It is a loss to us all that film cameras were not present to record his "That was unlucky" when scores were compared.

The next unrewarded excellent defence comes from the 1981 Bermuda Bowl:

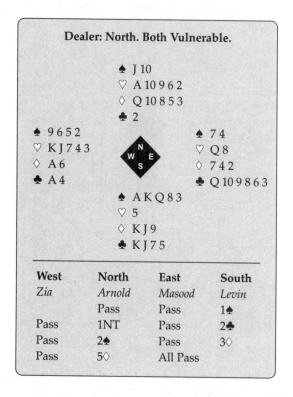

**Dealer: North. Both Vulnerable.**

|  | ♠ J 10 |  |
|  | ♡ A 10 9 6 2 |  |
|  | ◇ Q 10 8 5 3 |  |
|  | ♣ 2 |  |
| ♠ 9 6 5 2 | | ♠ 7 4 |
| ♡ K J 7 4 3 | | ♡ Q 8 |
| ◇ A 6 | | ◇ 7 4 2 |
| ♣ A 4 | | ♣ Q 10 9 8 6 3 |
|  | ♠ A K Q 8 3 |  |
|  | ♡ 5 |  |
|  | ◇ K J 9 |  |
|  | ♣ K J 7 5 |  |

| West | North | East | South |
|------|-------|------|-------|
| *Zia* | *Arnold* | *Masood* | *Levin* |
|  | Pass | Pass | 1♠ |
| Pass | 1NT | Pass | 2♣ |
| Pass | 2♠ | Pass | 3◇ |
| Pass | 5◇ | All Pass | |

Zia Mahmood led the unbid suit, hearts, and must have been surprised to see a chunky ♡A-10-9-x-x appear in the dummy. Bobby Levin won with the ace and played a club to the jack and ace. A second round of hearts forced declarer to ruff and Levin now headed for a cross-ruff. After cashing the ♣K and dummy's two spades, he ruffed a heart with the ◇J.

When another club was led from the South hand the key moment had been reached. If Zia had idly discarded, declarer would have scored a low trump in dummy, ruffed another heart and succeeded easily. No, Zia ruffed in with the ◇6, overruffed with the ◇8. Levin ruffed dummy's last heart with the ◇K and led a fourth round of clubs. Again it would have been fatal for Zia to discard. He made no mistake. He ruffed with the ◊A and led a spade, promoting East's ◊7-4-2, which lay over dummy's ◊Q-10-5. One down!

A bundle of IMPs to Pakistan, then? No, at the other table, after a similar start, Ahmed Nisar jumped to 4♠ at his third turn. Again a heart was led, won with the ace. Declarer could have made the game by drawing trumps and clearing the diamonds, but this needs the ◊A to be doubleton. Nisar led a club to jack and ace, ruffing the heart return. He then cashed the ♣K and made the mistake of leading a third round of clubs, allowing West to throw a diamond. Nisar ruffed the club in dummy and, belatedly, played a diamond. Eric Rodwell forced declarer in hearts again and declarer had lost control. He tried to draw trumps, finding a 4-2 break, and turned to the diamonds. When Rodwell ruffed the second round, declarer never made a diamond trick. He was two down for a 3-IMP loss.

Look back at the full diagram. Declarer needed only one diamond trick to bring his total to ten (five trump tricks, the ♣K and two club ruffs, the ♡A and one diamond). He should therefore have played a diamond after ruffing the second round of hearts. Whether or not Rodwell holds up the ◊A, the defenders would be powerless.

Zia lost 3 IMPs, despite his scintillating defence, but sometimes the loss is more. The hard-suffering declarer on the next deal was Charles Goren:

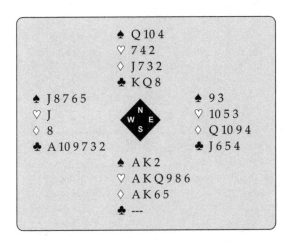

He arrived in 6♡ on those splendid South cards and West led the jack of trumps. Goren drew trumps in three rounds and cashed the two top diamonds, disappointed to see West show out on the second round. He now needed two entries in the dummy, to establish a club winner and then use it for a diamond discard. Goren cashed the ♠A and played a low spade to the ten! When the finesse won, he ran the♣K to West's ace, discarding his cumbersome ♠K. With only black cards remaining, West had to give the lead to one of dummy's black queens and both diamond losers went away.

This was truly a masterful performance, but not a very profitable one in terms of IMPs. At the other table, South attempted a contract of 7♡. West led an 'insulting' ♣A and declarer quickly took thirteen tricks!

Or so the story goes . . . The late Terence Reese, who has featured in this chapter already, used to view such deals with a weary eye. "If you believe that, you'll believe anything," he would say. Certainly the deal has the air of a construction about it. Mind you, we are reluctant to express open doubt about its veracity. Charles Goren was a masterful player, well capable of such a play.

You make a vulnerable 3NT on a combined total of 23 points. Would you expect to gain IMPs? Sorry, you're booked for an 11-IMP loss.

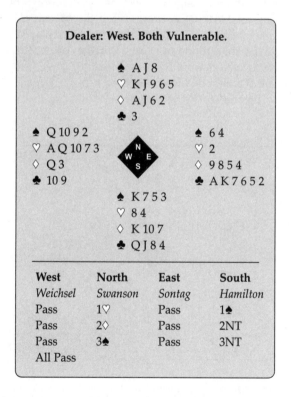

### Dealer: West. Both Vulnerable.

```
                    ♠ A J 8
                    ♡ K J 9 6 5
                    ◇ A J 6 2
                    ♣ 3
     ♠ Q 10 9 2                    ♠ 6 4
     ♡ A Q 10 7 3                  ♡ 2
     ◇ Q 3                         ◇ 9 8 5 4
     ♣ 10 9                        ♣ A K 7 6 5 2
                    ♠ K 7 5 3
                    ♡ 8 4
                    ◇ K 10 7
                    ♣ Q J 8 4
```

| West | North | East | South |
|------|-------|------|-------|
| *Weichsel* | *Swanson* | *Sontag* | *Hamilton* |
| Pass | 1♡ | Pass | 1♠ |
| Pass | 2◇ | Pass | 2NT |
| Pass | 3♣ | Pass | 3NT |
| All Pass | | | |

The deal comes from a 1978 Rosenblum match between Sontag and Blumenthal. At his second turn Fred Hamilton had to choose between a straightforward preference to 2♡ or the overbid of 2NT. He opted for the overbid and was soon installed in 3NT.

Peter Weichsel led the ♣10 and Alan Sontag allowed this to run, hoping that the lead was from ♣10-9-x and that five club tricks could be taken when West next gained the lead. Hamilton won and played a heart to the nine, winning the trick. After a diamond to the ten and queen, West exited passively with a diamond. A heart to the jack saw East pitching a club. Declarer cashed the remaining diamonds and West threw the ♣9. There was no longer any need to finesse in spades. Declarer crossed to his ♠K and simply led the ♣Q to East's king, forcing East to surrender a ninth trick in one of the black suits. This was the auction at the other table:

| West | North | East | South |
|------|-------|------|-------|
| *Becker* | *Lipsitz* | *Rubin* | *Silverman* |
| Pass | 1♡ | Pass | 1♠ |
| Pass | 2◇ | Pass | 2♡ |
| Pass | Pass | 3♣ | Dbl |
| All Pass | | | |

Neil Silverman gave simple preference and Ira Rubin chose an unlucky moment to protect. He went for 1100 and his side lost 11 IMPs instead of gaining 10 IMPs.

As always, we like to end the chapter with a bang. Here is a deal where the 'brilliancy unrewarded' theme is featured twice. It comes from the round-robin stage of the 1991 Bermuda Bowl:

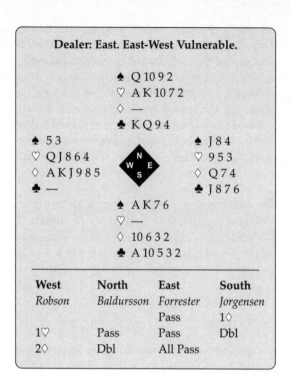

**Dealer: East. East-West Vulnerable.**

|  | ♠ Q 10 9 2 |  |
|---|---|---|
|  | ♡ A K 10 7 2 |  |
|  | ◇ — |  |
|  | ♣ K Q 9 4 |  |

| ♠ 5 3 | | ♠ J 8 4 |
| ♡ Q J 8 6 4 | | ♡ 9 5 3 |
| ◇ A K J 9 8 5 | | ◇ Q 7 4 |
| ♣ — | | ♣ J 8 7 6 |

|  | ♠ A K 7 6 |  |
|---|---|---|
|  | ♡ — |  |
|  | ◇ 10 6 3 2 |  |
|  | ♣ A 10 5 3 2 |  |

| West | North | East | South |
|---|---|---|---|
| *Robson* | *Baldursson* | *Forrester* | *Jorgensen* |
|  |  | Pass | 1◇ |
| 1♡ | Pass | Pass | Dbl |
| 2◇ | Dbl | All Pass |  |

Playing in 1♡ doubled, Andrew Robson might well have gone for 800.
He neatly escaped this fate by bidding 2◇ in front of the penalty-passer
and this set Baldursson quite a bidding problem. He elected to double, to
show that he held a penalty pass of 1♡, and there was no further bidding.
Robson must have been well pleased to concede only 200 with a small
slam in either black suit easy for North-South.

At the other table, Tony Sowter and Roman Smolski attempted the
grand:

| West | North | East | South |
|---|---|---|---|
| *Jonsson* | *Smolski* | *Arnarsson* | *Sowter* |
|  |  | Pass | 1♣ |
| 1◇ | 1♡ | Pass | 1♠ |
| 2◇ | 4NT | Pass | 5♣ |
| Pass | 7♣ | All Pass |  |

Roman Smolski's 4NT was Roman Key-card for spades, the response
showing three key-cards. Confident from West's bidding that one of
these would not be the ◇A, Smolski bid a grand in clubs.

Tony Sowter ruffed the ◇A lead and then cashed the king of trumps, getting the bad news. Since drawing trumps would leave him one trick short, he headed for a cross-ruff. He cashed ♡A-K, throwing two spades, and ruffed a heart. The ♠A-K were followed by a second diamond ruff and the ♣Q, East following. When Sowter led another heart from dummy, Gudmundur Arnarsson ruffed in order to force South's ♣10. After ruffing another diamond, Sowter called for another heart. Arnarsson ruffed again, forcing the ace of trumps from declarer and the grand slam was defeated. East could not be denied a trump trick. So Robson's coup, which seemed destined to gain a hefty swing, lost 6 IMPs.

On the very same deal Lynn Deas, playing for USA-2 in the Venice Cup, became the only declarer to land the club grand slam without a defensive error. She also ruffed the ◇A and cashed the ♣K getting the bad news. She cashed ♡A-K, pitching a spade and a diamond, and ruffed a third heart. She then cashed three spade tricks, ending in dummy, and led a heart in this position:

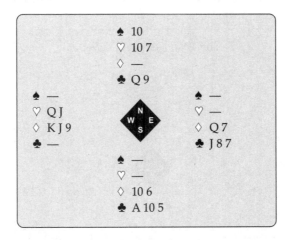

If East discards, declarer will ruff low and cross-ruff for thirteen tricks. So East ruffed with the seven, overruffed with the ten. Deas crossed to dummy with another diamond ruff, and again played a heart. East had no answer. When she ruffed with the eight, Deas overruffed with the ace and played a trump to the queen, drawing East's last trump. The thirteenth trick was dummy's master spade.

Lynn Deas did not win a single IMP from her brilliant performance, In fact she lost 2 IMPs because at the other table South played in the unbeatable 7♠. Bridge can be a tough game!

# 23
# Enough to Make Anyone Cry

I f ever there was a bridge hand to bring tears to the eye it was the very last deal of the 2003 Bermuda Bowl final. USA faced Italy, as had been the case in so many previous finals, and in the middle of the penultimate segment the Americans found themselves some 60 IMPs in the lead. Italy fought back with a string of wonderful results and, with only two boards of the final remaining, had moved into a near-impregnable lead of 21 IMPs.

On the penultimate board Hamman and Soloway did well to stop in 4♡. Bocchi and Duboin reached 5♡ and went one down very unluckily when trumps broke badly and declarer misguessed which black-suit finesse to take. The Italians lost 10 IMPs but still led by 11 IMPs. The players then drew their cards for the last board, one that was to provide perhaps the most dramatic climax in the history of the game:

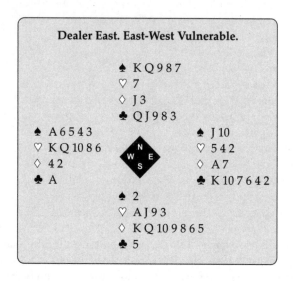

**Dealer East. East-West Vulnerable.**

```
                  ♠ K Q 9 8 7
                  ♡ 7
                  ♦ J 3
                  ♣ Q J 9 8 3
    ♠ A 6 5 4 3              ♠ J 10
    ♡ K Q 10 8 6            ♡ 5 4 2
    ♦ 4 2                    ♦ A 7
    ♣ A                      ♣ K 10 7 6 4 2
                  ♠ 2
                  ♡ A J 9 3
                  ♦ K Q 10 9 8 6 5
                  ♣ 5
```

In the Closed Room Norberto Bocchi and Giorgio Duboin had, for the second board in succession, strayed too high. They had bid to 4♡ on the East-West cards and not made the most of the play, going four down vulnerable for a loss of 400. To tie the match, and take it to extra boards, the American East-West pair needed to score another 100-190 points (for example, by making 2♡ for +110). If they scored less than +100, they would lose the match; if they scored +200 or more, they would win the match.

This was the auction in the Open Room :

| West | North | East | South |
|------|-------|------|-------|
| Soloway | Versace | Hamman | Lauria |
| | | Pass | 1◊ |
| 2◊ | Dbl | 2♡ | 3◊ |
| Pass | Pass | 3♡ | 5◊ |
| Dbl | All Pass | | |

West's 2◊ was a Michaels cue-bid, showing length in both majors. Bob Hamman was surely destined to go down in 3♡ and the American spectators in the Vu-Graph theatre were fearing the worst. Then, out of the blue, Lorenzo Lauria made the amazing bid of 5◊! He could place his partner with a shortage in hearts, yes, but there was no guarantee of sufficient diamond support to take the heart ruffs that would be needed. In any case, he had already shown a good diamond suit with his rebid of 3◊ and partner had made no move towards game. Paul Soloway lost no time in doubling and the match had swung back to the Americans. Lauria would now have to escape for only one down to tie the match and this seemed quite impossible.

A trump lead would have prevented any heart ruffs, taking the doubled game three down. Very reasonably, Soloway chose to lead the ♣A with the aim of scoring a ruff in the suit. A trump switch would still have been effective but he next attempted to put his partner on lead by switching to the ♡Q. Lauria disappointed him by winning with the ace. He then continued with the ♡J, hoping that East had started with ♡10-x-x and two heart ruffs would bring down the ten.

Soloway covered with the ♡K and declarer ruffed in dummy. Lauria returned to his hand by ruffing a club with the ◊8. He then ruffed another heart in dummy but the ♡10 failed to appear. With an apparently certain loser in each of the four suits, the Italians were booked for a further loss of 300 on the board. The Bermuda Bowl was heading in a westerly direction across the Atlantic. Or was it? The drama was not yet over.

After taking his second heart ruff, Lauria exited from dummy with the ♠K. Soloway, sitting West, won with the ♠A and these cards were left:

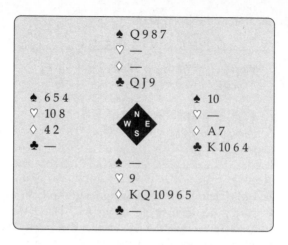

Soloway needed only to cash the ♡10 to win the Bermuda Bowl. Uncertain of the position, and to the amazement of the Vu-Graph commentators and everyone watching in the theatre, he played a spade! The match was now surely tied, since Lauria could win with dummy's ♠Q and discard his losing heart.

Versace was not sitting in the North chair. He had left the table early, as on previous sessions when he had been dummy on the last board, to score up with his team-mates. Lauria had therefore been reaching across the table to play the cards from the dummy. On this occasion he leaned forward and played . . . the ♠7! Hamman covered with the ♠10 and the contract was two down. America had gained 12 IMPs and won the match by 1 IMP.

What on earth had happened? Lauria, understandably exhausted after playing for so many days, had expected Soloway to cash his heart winner. He had not registered that a spade had been led and had merely discarded the spot-card in dummy that was nearest his thumb. Had this happened to be a club, it would have been an illegal play. He would then have been alerted to the fact that a spade had been led and would have been able to change his card to the ♠Q.

When Lauria saw, to his horror, that West had led a spade, he made a belated attempt to change his play from the dummy. The Director ruled that the ♠7 had been touched and was therefore a played card. The Italians appealed the decision, although it's hard to see on what basis, and the Appeals Committee duly confirmed the Director's ruling.

After recovering so heroically from a 60-IMP deficit, it was a tragic ending for the Italians and for Lauria in particular. Suppose that Lauria had played dummy's ♠Q, though, and the Italians had eventually won the trophy on the extra boards. Think how shattered Soloway would have been! His failure to cash a winner on the final board of regular time would then have cost the USA the Bermuda Bowl.

---

# 24
# Cardinal Sins:
# the ruff-and-discard

All bridge players remember the moment in their playing career when they were ranked as a 'beginner'. For some individuals this stage lasts quite some time, even forever. Beginners commit all sorts of errors and blunders and are duly chastised by partners, opponents or kibitzers. One of the worst sins they can commit in defence is to give declarer a ruff-and-discard, or ruff-and-sluff as North Americans call it.

Memories of performing this dreadful act, and the consequences, are deeply ingrained. Some players are never again able to commit such a sin, even when it is best course of action as in our first deal. It arose in the Transnational Teams event at the Hammamet 1997 World Championships:

---

**Dealer: South. East-West Vulnerable.**

```
                ♠ 84
                ♡ A K 2
                ◇ 6 3
                ♣ A K J 6 5 2
♠ K 9 5                          ♠ 10 7 3
♡ Q 8 6 5          N             ♡ 10
◇ J 9 8 7 2    W       E         ◇ A Q 10 5 4
♣ 9               S             ♣ Q 7 4 3
                ♠ A Q J 6 2
                ♡ J 9 7 4 3
                ◇ K
                ♣ 10 8
```

| West | North | East | South |
|------|-------|------|-------|
| *Møller* | | *Schaffer* | |
| | | | 1♠ |
| Pass | 2♣ | Pass | 2♡ |
| Pass | 3◇ | Dbl | 3♡ |
| Pass | 4♡ | All Pass | |

---

Guided by the lead-directing double of the fourth-suit bid, Kirsten Steen Møller led the ◇2. Lauge Schaffer took his ace, the king appearing from

---

South, and continued the suit, declarer ruffing. A trump to the ace, dropping East's ten was followed by a losing finesse of the ♠Q. Suppose you had been sitting West. What would you have done next?

It was fairly obvious that the defenders had no further tricks in the side suits. To bolster the prospects of her remaining Q-8-6 in the trump suit, Møller led a third diamond, offering a ruff-and-discard! Declarer had no counter to this. If he ruffed with dummy's ♡2, he could draw another of West's trumps with the king but West was certain to score two more tricks with her ♡Q-8.

A diamond return at Trick 5, giving a ruff-and-discard, was the only way to beat the contract! If you're short of something to do this evening . . . you can work out how declarer can make the contract on a spade return.

In the other room the West player preferred to lead his singleton club. He did receive a club ruff eventually but Sabine Auken made ten tricks by finessing against the ♡Q on the second round. It's an instructive reminder that when you hold four good trumps you should generally prefer a forcing game to searching for a ruff.

There is an ancient Greek adage that can be roughly translated as 'A wise man is one who doesn't make the same mistake twice'. Much as both the authors admire the ancient Greeks (especially Nikos, who is Greek if not yet ancient), we admit that the adage was coined before bridge was invented. There are several situations where a repeated lapse into the unmentionable sin of a ruff-and-discard is a very wise thing to do! Take, for example, this deal from the 2002 US Nationals in Houston:

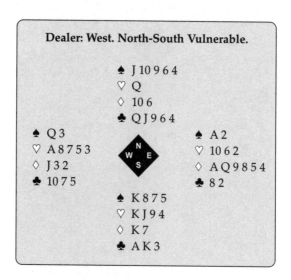

**Dealer: West. North-South Vulnerable.**

|  | ♠ J 10 9 6 4 |  |
|---|---|---|
|  | ♡ Q |  |
|  | ◇ 10 6 |  |
|  | ♣ Q J 9 6 4 |  |
| ♠ Q 3 |  | ♠ A 2 |
| ♡ A 8 7 5 3 | | ♡ 10 6 2 |
| ◇ J 3 2 | | ◇ A Q 9 8 5 4 |
| ♣ 10 7 5 | | ♣ 8 2 |
|  | ♠ K 8 7 5 |  |
|  | ♡ K J 9 4 |  |
|  | ◇ K 7 |  |
|  | ♣ A K 3 |  |

| West | North | East | South |
|------|-------|------|-------|
| *Pearce* | | *Glubok* | |
| Pass | Pass | 1♦ | 1NT |
| Pass | 2♡ | Pass | 3♠ |
| Pass | 4♠ | All Pass | |

South played in four spades after overcalling 1NT and breaking partner's transfer response. Pollyanna Pearce led a diamond to partner's ace and Brian Glubok returned the suit. To make the contract now, against best defence, declarer must lead the ♣3 to dummy's queen and play a trump to the king. Sensing no particular danger, he followed the more intuitive path of leading a heart. Pearce rose with the ace and asked herself this question: "Why did declarer play a heart rather than the ace of trumps?" The obvious answer was that he did not hold the ace of trumps and needed to enter dummy to lead towards his king.

In that case Pearce could see a way to beat the contract. At Trick 4 she led a third round of diamonds, conceding a ruff-and-discard. Declarer ruffed in the dummy and discarded the ♡9. When he led a trump from dummy, Glubok rose with the ace and led a fourth round of diamonds, conceding yet another ruff-and-discard. It was the end of the road for declarer. He could not prevent West's bare queen of trumps from being promoted.

Perhaps you are a tough customer and refuse to be impressed by the double ruff-and-sluff. How about three ruff-and-discards in the same deal and, what is more, performed by the same defender? The player concerned was the legendary Fritzi Gordon. The deal arose in a World Pairs Championship in the early 1960s, when she was partnering the equally famous Rixi Markus:

---

```
                    ♠ J 8 7 5 4 2
                    ♡ J
                    ◇ 8 4
                    ♣ J 6 4 3
  ♠ A Q                              ♠ 10 9 3
  ♡ 7 5 4              N             ♡ 10 8 3
  ◇ J 9 6 3 2      W     E           ◇ A K 10 5
  ♣ K 9 2              S             ♣ 8 7 5
                    ♠ K 6
                    ♡ A K Q 9 6 2
                    ◇ Q 7
                    ♣ A Q 10
```

| West | North | East | South |
|------|-------|------|-------|
| *Gordon* | | *Markus* | |
| | | | 2NT |
| Pass | 4♡ | Pass | 4♠ |
| All Pass | | | |

North's 4♡ was a Texas transfer. This was not one of the many deals in history where the opener forgot the meaning of the bid and passed. No, perhaps alerted by his own splendid heart holding, he completed the transfer and 4♠ became the final contract.

Fritzi Gordon led the ◇3 and Rixi pocketed two diamond tricks. She then returned a club to the ten and king. Many partnerships would be happy with +200 for two down but it was a pairs event and Fritzi was looking for the third undertrick. When she played a diamond (the first ruff-and-discard), South ruffed in the dummy and played a low trump to the king and ace. A fourth round of diamonds was ruffed in the dummy and declarer now needed to reach his hand to lead a trump towards dummy's jack. He advanced the ♡J, overtaken with the queen, and led the ♠6 from his hand to West's queen. A fifth round of diamonds, the third ruff-and-discard, promoted East's ♠10. That was three down and a clear top for the ladies.

When Nikos first wrote about ruff-and-discards (in *Bridge Plus* magazine), he ended by saying: "Despite a diligent search, I have not found a deal with four ruff-and-discards. I doubt if I ever will." No sooner had the issue been published when the renowned French double-dummy composer, Damien Lescot, sent in this elegant construction:

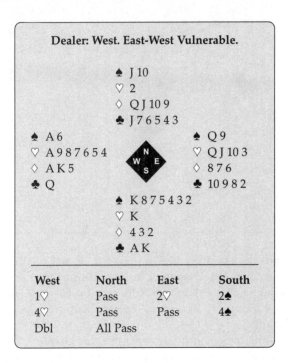

**Dealer: West. East-West Vulnerable.**

|  |  |  |
|---|---|---|
|  | ♠ J 10 |  |
|  | ♡ 2 |  |
|  | ◇ Q J 10 9 |  |
|  | ♣ J 7 6 5 4 3 |  |
| ♠ A 6 | | ♠ Q 9 |
| ♡ A 9 8 7 6 5 4 | | ♡ Q J 10 3 |
| ◇ A K 5 | | ◇ 8 7 6 |
| ♣ Q | | ♣ 10 9 8 2 |
|  | ♠ K 8 7 5 4 3 2 |  |
|  | ♡ K |  |
|  | ◇ 4 3 2 |  |
|  | ♣ A K |  |

| West | North | East | South |
|------|-------|------|-------|
| 1♡ | Pass | 2♡ | 2♠ |
| 4♡ | Pass | Pass | 4♠ |
| Dbl | All Pass | | |

Expecting the heart game to succeed, South sacrifices in 4♠. This contract is one down off the top, so the defenders' target is to beat the contract by two tricks. How can this be done?

West successfully cashes the ♡A at Trick 1. You will not fall off your chair when you hear that the next move West must make is to lead a second round of hearts, giving a ruff-and-discard. Declarer cannot afford to waste one of dummy's trump honours (this would promote a second trump trick for East's ♠Q-9), so he ruffs in the South hand. He must now attempt to reach dummy in diamonds, so that he can run the ♠J through East's queen.

West rises with the king on the first round of diamonds and . . . yes . . . concedes another ruff-and-discard in hearts. Declarer ruffs in his hand and leads another diamond. West wins with the ace and leads yet another heart, conceding a third ruff-and-discard. Declarer ruffs in the South hand and reaches dummy with a diamond at long last, both defenders following suit. These cards remain:

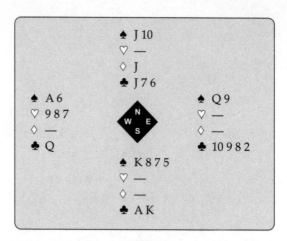

Declarer leads the ♠J, covered by the queen, king and ace. Triumphantly, West leads another heart, giving a ruff-and-discard for the fourth time. This promotes East's ♠9 and the penalty rises to 300. It was the only way to beat the contract by two tricks. (Many thanks to Damien for this splendid deal.)

What is the lesson to be drawn from this chapter? The ruff-and-discard is not always a sin. Indeed, sometimes it may turn out to be a virtue. Isn't it the same with all sins?

# 25
# Doubles That Turned to Gold

**B**ack in Chapter 20 we saw some doubles that were technically sound but ended in disaster. It is time to look at the opposite end of the spectrum – at some truly awful doubles that somehow or other ended in a big triumph. How can that happen? Perhaps the double induces the opponents to run to a worse spot. Alternatively a declarer may be bamboozled into adopting an inferior line of play. Let's see!

The first deal is from the 2002 Salsomaggiore European Championships:

**Dealer: North. East-West Vulnerable.**

|  |  |  |
|---|---|---|
|  | ♠ — |  |
|  | ♡ J 9 8 |  |
|  | ◊ K Q 5 4 3 2 |  |
|  | ♣ 9 8 7 4 |  |
| ♠ A 10 8 7 4 2 |  | ♠ 6 |
| ♡ 10 7 4 3 | W  N  E | ♡ A K 6 5 2 |
| ◊ 9 6 | S | ◊ J 10 8 7 |
| ♣ 10 |  | ♣ A 5 3 |
|  | ♠ K Q J 9 5 3 |  |
|  | ♡ Q |  |
|  | ◊ A |  |
|  | ♣ K Q J 6 2 |  |

| West | North | East | South |
|------|-------|------|-------|
| *Lauria* | *Harfouche* | *Versace* | *Eidi* |
|  | Pass | 1♡ | 2♡ |
| 4♡ | 4NT | Pass | 5♣ |
| Pass | Pass | Dbl | Pass |
| Pass | 5◊ | Dbl | 5♠ |
| Dbl | 5NT | Pass | 6♠ |
| Dbl | All Pass |  |  |

What would you have bid on the first round with that South hand? It is not usually right to employ Michaels when you hold a strong six-card major-suit because there is too much risk that partner will insist on the minor. Michel Eidi had chosen the right moment, though. With a four-card

---

discrepancy in the black suits opposite, 5♣ was cold and 4♠ had no play.

It is hard to explain Alfredo Versace's double of the club game, unless he thought that the bidding of a vulnerable game his way had set up a 'forcing pass' situation. His partner had already declined to double 5♣ and he himself had less defence than was to be expected for an opening bid. The apparently poor double was to turn to gold, however. Hoping that his partner held a 5-0-3-5 shape (or at worst 5-1-2-5), Gabriel Harfouche took it upon himself to rescue into 5◊. Versace had a more comfortable double of this contract, although not so comfortable as Lorenzo Lauria's subsequent doubles of 5♠ and 6♠! Eidi went four off doubled, for 800, losing 15 IMPs when he would have gained 4 IMPs by playing successfully in 5♣ doubled. (At the other table North made 5♣ undoubled.)

No-trump contracts are especially vulnerable to doubles which, even when unsound, may sow seeds of doubt. The next deal comes from the 2003 US Bridge Championship semi-final:

---

**Dealer: East. Both Vulnerable.**

```
                  ♠ J 8 7 6
                  ♡ J 9 7 5
                  ◊ K 10 9 3
                  ♣ A
  ♠ 9 2                          ♠ 10 5 4 3
  ♡ 6 3 2              N         ♡ A K Q 8 4
  ◊ Q 8 4          W     E       ◊ 5 2
  ♣ K 8 5 3 2         S          ♣ 9 7
                  ♠ A K Q
                  ♡ 10
                  ◊ A J 7 6
                  ♣ Q J 10 6 4
```

| West | North | East | South |
|------|-------|------|-------|
| *Levin* | *Wildavsky* | *Weinstein* | *Doub* |
|      |        | Pass | 1♣ |
| Pass | 1♡ | Pass | 1NT |
| Pass | 2♣ | Pass | 2◊ |
| Pass | 2♠ | Pass | 3NT |
| Pass | Pass | Dbl | 4♣ |
| All Pass |    |      |     |

---

If Steve Weinstein had held the ♡10 instead of the ♡8, he would have had a perfect lead-directing double of 3NT. Even with his lesser heart holding, a heart lead is the only one to give the defenders a chance of beating 3NT. East must duck the heart lead, maintaining communication with his partner. Declarer then has only eight top tricks and will have to guess correctly in diamonds to land the contract. Mind you, East would probably have opened 1♡ if he held the ◊Q in addition to his splendid heart suit, so declarer would probably guess the diamond suit correctly, ending with an overtrick.

As we see it, South had no reason whatsoever to run from 3NT doubled. His ♡10 was a potentially useful card and he had already defined his hand accurately. He went one down in the bizarre contract of 4♣, with game in diamonds an easy make. At the other table Bobby Wolff led a spade against North's 3NT and declarer set up the clubs to make the game. Another potentially faulty penalty double had netted a big swing.

On the next deal, from the 1997 Australian Open championship, a small slam in spades is cold for North-South and only an unlikely club lead will stop an overtrick. West did not find a club lead but his double of the small slam gained in an unexpected way. It caused declarer to take a losing line in the play.

---

**Dealer: South. North-South Vulnerable.**

```
                    ♠ A Q 3 2
                    ♡ 9 8 7 3
                    ◊ Q 7
                    ♣ K 9 7
  ♠ K 5                              ♠ 10 9
  ♡ A K J 6 2          N            ♡ Q 10 5 4
  ◊ 6              W       E         ◊ 10 8 2
  ♣ A J 4 3 2          S            ♣ Q 8 6 5
                    ♠ J 8 7 6 4
                    ♡ —
                    ◊ A K J 9 5 4 3
                    ♣ 10
```

| West | North | East | South |
|------|-------|------|-------|
|      | *Waradia* |  | *Munawar* |
|      |       |      | 1◊ |
| 1♡ | Dbl | 3♡ | 4♠ |
| 5♣ | Dbl | 5♡ | 5♠ |
| Pass | Pass | 6♡ | Pass |
| Pass | 6♠ | Pass | Pass |
| Dbl | All Pass |  |  |

---

Sawiruddin Munawar, an Indonesian international, ruffed the ♡A lead. He was convinced by East's vigorous bidding that East was short in trumps, a hypothesis corroborated by West's double. If West held ♠K-10-9 there was nothing to be done, but he could cater for a holding of ♠K-10-x or ♠K-9-x by starting with the ♠J. This he did. West covered with the king, dummy won with the ace and East produced the ten. Returning to hand with a heart ruff, declarer ran the eight of trumps . . . to East's now bare nine! East was quick to return a club and the small slam failed! Obviously, had declarer gone up with queen on the second round of trumps he would have made all thirteen tricks.

There was plenty of action when the deal was played in another match:

| West | North | East | South |
|------|-------|------|-------|
| *Weichsel* | *Braithwaite* | *Jacobus* | *Cornell* |
|      |       |      | 1♢ |
| 1♡ | Dbl | 3♡ | 4♡ |
| Dbl | Pass | Pass | 4♠ |
| 5♣ | 6♠ | 7♣ | 7♠ |
| Dbl | All Pass | | |

A wild auction ended with the New Zealand pair in a doubled grand slam. Michael Cornell surely realised that 7♠ would fail on a club lead, but on a heart lead there would be chances.

It is not every day that you find yourself on lead against a grand slam holding the king of trumps, an ace and an ace-king! What would you have led from that West hand? If there is any reason to lead the ♣A rather than a top heart we cannot see it. Peter Weichsel duly led the ♡A, ruffed by declarer. A trump to the queen, followed by the ace of trumps, dealt with that suit and Cornell was soon writing +2470 in his score-card. At the other table of this match North-South had collected +950 for a doubled overtrick in 5♢. So, Weichsel's opening lead, compared with a lead of the ♣A, had cost 32 IMPs.

We end at the 1993 Junior world championship in Aarhus, where a double of a cold game caused declarer to go astray in the play. Should he have done better? Watch as the play is described and see what you think.

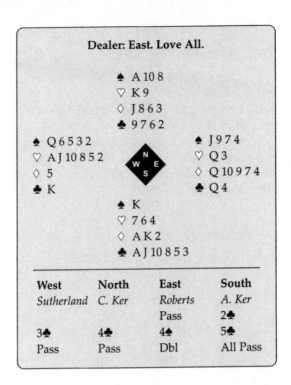

**Dealer: East. Love All.**

|  | ♠ A 10 8 |  |
|---|---|---|
|  | ♡ K 9 |  |
|  | ◊ J 8 6 3 |  |
|  | ♣ 9 7 6 2 |  |
| ♠ Q 6 5 3 2 |  | ♠ J 9 7 4 |
| ♡ A J 10 8 5 2 |  | ♡ Q 3 |
| ◊ 5 |  | ◊ Q 10 9 7 4 |
| ♣ K |  | ♣ Q 4 |
|  | ♠ K |  |
|  | ♡ 7 6 4 |  |
|  | ◊ A K 2 |  |
|  | ♣ A J 10 8 5 3 |  |

| West | North | East | South |
|---|---|---|---|
| *Sutherland* | *C. Ker* | *Roberts* | *A. Ker* |
|  |  | Pass | 2♣ |
| 3♣ | 4♣ | 4♠ | 5♣ |
| Pass | Pass | Dbl | All Pass |

South's 2♣ opening was natural, suggesting a six-card club suit. West's 3♣ showed a two-suiter in the majors. The eventual contract of 5♣, doubled by East, appears to be cold. The ♡A is onside and declarer's diamond loser can be thrown on the ♠A. How could declarer possibly go down?

West led a spade to declarer's bare king. Convinced by the final double that trumps would be 3-0, declarer aimed to reach dummy for a trump finesse. When he led a heart, West rose with the ace and returned another heart to dummy's king. The ♡Q appeared from East, suggesting that hearts might be 6-2. Declarer persisted with a trump finesse and when East won with the ♣K he led a third round of hearts, East overruffing the dummy. One down!

What did you make of that? Trumps might well have been 3-0 and declarer was right to attempt to deal with that situation. However, there was no need at all to lead the first round of trumps from dummy. At Trick 2, he should have led the ♣J from his hand. As it happens, a 2-1 trump break would come to light. Declarer could then draw the outstanding trump and make the contract easily. If trumps had been 3-0, as expected, he could have reverted to the original line, fighting his way to the ♡K to pick up East's remaining holding. North-South stopped in 4♣ at the other table, so declarer's misplay cost a net swing of 15 IMPs.

# 26
# The Amazing Discrepancy

Has it ever happened, in a top level event, that one North-South pair bid and made a grand slam while the other North-South pair stopped in a part-score? Yes, indeed. But not at the very top level. It was only a world championship semi-final rather than a final! This was the deal, with Sweden facing Italy in the 2002 Rosenblum Cup, contested in Montreal:

**Dealer: South. North-South Vulnerable.**

```
                 ♠ A Q
                 ♡ 6 5 4
                 ◇ Q 8 5
                 ♣ K 10 7 6 4
  ♠ 10 4 3                      ♠ 8 7 5
  ♡ 3                N          ♡ K 10 9 8 2
  ◇ J 10 9 7 4 3   W   E        ◇ A K 6 2
  ♣ J 9 8            S          ♣ 5
                 ♠ K J 9 6 2
                 ♡ A Q J 7
                 ◇ —
                 ♣ A Q 3 2
```

| West | North | East | South |
|------|-------|------|-------|
| *Versace* | *Fredin* | *Lauria* | *Lindkvist* |
| | | | 1♣ |
| Pass | 1NT | 2♡ | 2♠ |
| Pass | 3♣ | Pass | 4◇ |
| Pass | 4♠ | Pass | 5◇ |
| Pass | 7♣ | All Pass | |

The Swedish South player opened with a strong club and North's 1NT showed a balanced hand of 8-12 points, without four spades. The Italian East entered the auction, as players do, and the next two Swedish bids were natural. South then jumped to 4◇, agreeing clubs and showing a diamond shortage. North's 4♠ showed a spade control but denied a control in hearts. South's 5◇ was a grand slam try and therefore, by inference, showed first-round control in hearts as well as in diamonds.

North had heard enough and with three prime cards in the black suits he leapt to the grand slam. Excellent bidding and there were no problems in the play. No doubt the Swedes would have stopped in a small slam, had East not telegraphed the position of the ♡K with his overcall. The Italian East-West must have been apprehensive of a poor board.

Such fears proved to be well grounded in a big way when this was the auction at the other table:

| West | North | East | South |
|------|-------|------|-------|
| Nystrom | Duboin | Bertheau | Bocchi |
| | | | 1♠ |
| Pass | 2♣ | Pass | 2♡ |
| Pass | 2NT | Pass | 3♣ |
| All Pass | | | |

North's 2♣ response was artificial. It did not promise clubs and merely showed any hand of game-invitational strength or better. His 2NT rebid suggested around 11 points and was non-forcing. South rated his 3♣ as forcing. North was equally sure about the nature of this bid: it was non-forcing. Not a particularly complicated sequence, you would have thought, particularly for players at this level. How do you rate this sequence? South's 3♣ was introducing a new suit, remember, since North had not yet shown his club suit. If you play the forcing 1NT response to one of a major, the sequence is analogous to:

| West | North | East | South |
|------|-------|------|-------|
| | | | 1♠ |
| Pass | 1NT* | Pass | 2♡ |
| Pass | 2NT | Pass | 3♣ |
| All Pass | | | |
| *forcing | | | |

It seems best that 3♣ should be forcing. 3♣ and 3◊ are important natural bids to have available when you are strong and need to investigate the best place to play. On a weak 5-4-0-4 shape, you can simply pass. Some would say that South should have cleared the air with a leap to 4♣. There was no need to do this if 3♣ was forcing. Indeed, if North had considerable values in diamonds South would have been happy to play in 3NT. Our preferences, in descending order are: (a) 3♣ is forcing, (b) 3♣ is non-forcing, and (c) the situation has never been discussed, even though we are playing in a world championship!

We said that this deal arose in a world championship semi-final. In the other match the very same deal led to some amazing exchanges. The discrepancy between the two contracts was less but still one side bid to a slam and the other stopped in game. This was the less ambitious auction:

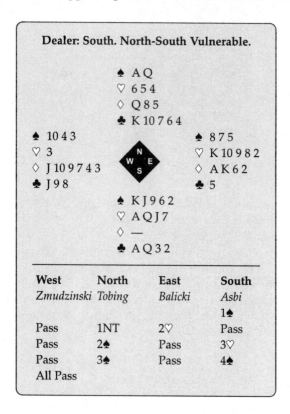

Dealer: South. North-South Vulnerable.

|  | ♠ A Q |  |
|  | ♡ 6 5 4 |  |
|  | ◇ Q 8 5 |  |
|  | ♣ K 10 7 6 4 |  |

| ♠ 10 4 3 | | ♠ 8 7 5 |
| ♡ 3 | | ♡ K 10 9 8 2 |
| ◇ J 10 9 7 4 3 | | ◇ A K 6 2 |
| ♣ J 9 8 | | ♣ 5 |

|  | ♠ K J 9 6 2 |  |
|  | ♡ A Q J 7 |  |
|  | ◇ — |  |
|  | ♣ A Q 3 2 |  |

| West | North | East | South |
|------|-------|------|-------|
| *Zmudzinski* | *Tobing* | *Balicki* | *Asbi* |
|  |  |  | 1♠ |
| Pass | 1NT | 2♡ | Pass |
| Pass | 2♠ | Pass | 3♡ |
| Pass | 3♠ | Pass | 4♠ |
| All Pass |  |  |  |

Most pairs would play a penalty double of intervention after a start of 1♠ – 1NT. It seems this bid was not available to South. He passed on his 18-count, no doubt hoping that his partner would re-open with a take-out double that could be passed for penalties. North had an awkward rebid. Eleven points, yes, but what limit bid could he make? With one eye on his unimpressive x-x-x in the suit that had been overcalled, he eventually settled for the distinct underbid of 2♠. South rose from the dead with a cue bid of 3♡ and the partnership eventually limped into 4♠. It is hard to understand why North did not bid 4♣ over 3♡. Perhaps he was simply leaving room for partner to bid a delayed 3NT.

The fireworks came at the other table, where Leandro Burgay (South) opened with his artificial strong bid of 1◇.

| West | North | East | South |
|------|-------|------|-------|
| *Lasut* | *Mariani* | *Manoppo* | *Burgay* |
| | | | 1◊ |
| 3◊ | 3NT | Pass | 4◊ |
| Pass | 4♡ | Pass | 5◊ |
| Pass | 5♠ | Pass | 6♡ |
| Pass | Pass | Dbl!! | 6♠ |
| All Pass | | | |

Perhaps hoping for a mention in this book (in our weak overcall chapter), Henky Lasut entered with 3◊. North bid a natural 3NT and South sought a fit somewhere with his cue bid of 4◊. What would you have bid next on those North cards?

Carlo Mariani took the view that partner was asking him to choose between the major suits. He chose 4♡ and then had to interpret the continuation of 5◊. More than once, years ago, players have passed such repeat cue bids, concluding that the opponents' overcall had been psychic and that partner really wanted to play in the suit. Mariani did not make that mistake. Correctly reading that his partner was agreeing hearts and looking for a slam in the suit, he cue-bid 5♠. Burgay signed off in 6♡, a contract that was doomed to defeat by the bad trump break.

The auction was not yet over! Incredibly, for a player of his stature, Manoppo made a greedy double of the heart slam. Burgay was quick to retreat to 6♠ and that contract was made with an overtrick. Playing in hearts, declarer has to follow an unusual line even to make just ten tricks after a diamond lead. (He must abandon trumps after one finesse and play on the black suits.) Manoppo had therefore swapped a plus score of at least 200, had he passed out 6♡, with a minus score of 1460.

Even at this awesome level of the game the four pairs had managed contracts of *part-score, game, small slam and grand slam* on a single board. It gives us all hope!

# 27
# He Knew What He Was Doing!

Have you ever had the opportunity to let the opponents play at the two level, but you re-opened the bidding and they then bid to a grand slam? It happened in the 2003 match between the House of Lords and a Cambridge University graduates team:

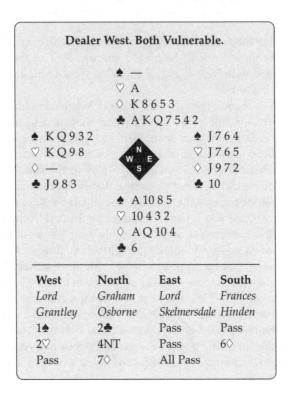

Dealer West. Both Vulnerable.

```
                    ♠ —
                    ♡ A
                    ◇ K 8 6 5 3
                    ♣ A K Q 7 5 4 2
  ♠ K Q 9 3 2                      ♠ J 7 6 4
  ♡ K Q 9 8          N             ♡ J 7 6 5
  ◇ —            W       E         ◇ J 9 7 2
  ♣ J 9 8 3          S             ♣ 10
                    ♠ A 10 8 5
                    ♡ 10 4 3 2
                    ◇ A Q 10 4
                    ♣ 6
```

| West | North | East | South |
|------|-------|------|-------|
| *Lord* | *Graham* | *Lord* | *Frances* |
| *Grantley* | *Osborne* | *Skelmersdale* | *Hinden* |
| 1♠ | 2♣ | Pass | Pass |
| 2♡ | 4NT | Pass | 6◇ |
| Pass | 7◇ | All Pass | |

Graham Osborne overcalled 2♣ and was alarmed to hear two passes. When Lord Grantley protected with 2♡, Osborne rebid 4NT to show a massive hand in the minors. Frances Hinden jumped to 6◇ and Osborne raised to the grand!

The play would be easy on a spade lead but Lord Grantley led a top heart, removing a key entry to the dummy. Hinden won with dummy's bare ace and played a trump to the ace, West showing out. Suppose you had been the declarer. How would you have played the contract from this point?

Declarer went one down at the table but thirteen tricks can be made by an unusual form of play. You cross to the ♣A and play the ♣K. East does best to discard and you throw a heart. You then ruff a club with the ◊4 and return to dummy with a heart ruff. This position remains:

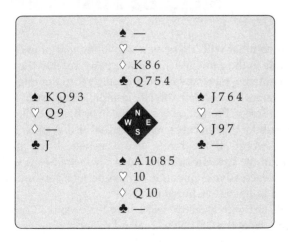

If you finesse the ten of trumps next, you will lose control and go down. Instead you must lead good clubs through East, a technique called 'using a side suit as substitute trumps'. If East refuses to ruff at any stage, you will discard the four major-suit losers from your hand and eventually score the last three tricks in trumps, finessing the ten. If instead East ruffs one of the clubs, you will overruff with the ◊10 and play the ◊Q. You then return to dummy with a spade ruff to draw the last trump. That's thirteen tricks without using the ♠A!

As we mentioned, the original declarer followed a different line and went one down, so Lord Grantley knew what he was doing when he re-opened the bidding with 2♡. Instead of writing 170 in the minus column, for 2♣ made with four overtricks, he entered 100 in the plus column for defeating the diamond grand slam. If only we could all display such excellent judgment.

# 28
# And, Yea, the Last
# Shall Be First

If you are familiar with chess, you will know that promotion plays a crucial role in the game. When a lowly pawn reaches the eighth rank it is promoted, almost always to a queen, i.e. to the mightiest piece. Most chess games are decided, directly or indirectly, by such a promotion or the threat thereof. Promotion is essential in bridge as well, although its presence is subtler than in chess, more gradual also. A chess pawn jumps in one fell swoop all the ranks, like a private being promoted to commander in the battlefield. In bridge a lowly spot-card will only get promoted by successive elimination of its superiors, very much like what happens in administrative bureaucracies.

We will start with a pretty deal where the promoted card is a hefty jack. It comes from the 2001 New Zealand national congress:

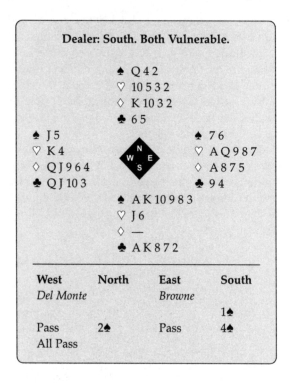

```
           Dealer: South. Both Vulnerable.
                    ♠ Q 4 2
                    ♡ 10 5 3 2
                    ◇ K 10 3 2
                    ♣ 6 5
   ♠ J 5                          ♠ 7 6
   ♡ K 4              N           ♡ A Q 9 8 7
   ◇ Q J 9 6 4    W     E         ◇ A 8 7 5
   ♣ Q J 10 3        S            ♣ 9 4
                    ♠ A K 10 9 8 3
                    ♡ J 6
                    ◇ —
                    ♣ A K 8 7 2
```

| West | North | East | South |
|------|-------|------|-------|
| *Del Monte* | | *Browne* | |
| | | | 1♠ |
| Pass | 2♠ | Pass | 4♠ |
| All Pass | | | |

Declarer was playing Precision, so his 1♠ bid showed fewer than 16 points. (Having said that, he was surely worth a 1♣ bid anyway.) Ishmael

---

Del Monte led the ♣Q and declarer won in his hand. A second high club stood up and declarer led a third round of the suit, ruffing with dummy's queen. On this trick East discarded a heart. What should declarer do next?

When the cards lie as in the diagram you can make the contract by drawing trumps. The ♠J falls in two rounds and you lose just two hearts and one club. Declarer realised that his prospects were stronger if he ruffed the last club. East would have to overruff the dummy and the contract would then succeed also when East had started with ♠J-x-x.

Declarer reached his hand with a diamond ruff and ruffed the fourth round of clubs, East overruffing. A low heart from East would have worked well now but instead he cashed the ♡A. All eyes were now back on Del Monte. Was he half asleep, reaching for his ♡4? No, he was counting declarer's points. East had not been able to overruff the ♠Q on the third round of clubs, so it was reasonable to place declarer with the ace and king of trumps. Since he had also shown up with the ♣A and ♣K, he could not hold the ♡Q. Such a card would have taken his point total to 16, too much for a Precision 1♠ opening.

Placing East with the ♡Q, Del Monte cleverly unblocked his ♡K under the ace. Browne continued with the ♡Q and then led a third round of hearts, promoting West's ♠J. Without the unblock, there is no defence.

Now let's see how a lowly seven became promoted:

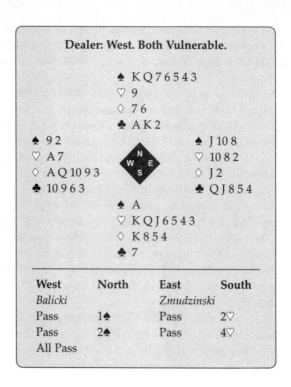

**Dealer: West. Both Vulnerable.**

|   |   |
|---|---|
| ♠ K Q 7 6 5 4 3 | |
| ♡ 9 | |
| ◇ 7 6 | |
| ♣ A K 2 | |

| | |
|---|---|
| ♠ 9 2 | ♠ J 10 8 |
| ♡ A 7 | ♡ 10 8 2 |
| ◇ A Q 10 9 3 | ◇ J 2 |
| ♣ 10 9 6 3 | ♣ Q J 8 5 4 |

|   |   |
|---|---|
| ♠ A | |
| ♡ K Q J 6 5 4 3 | |
| ◇ K 8 5 4 | |
| ♣ 7 | |

| West | North | East | South |
|------|-------|------|-------|
| *Balicki* | | *Zmudzinski* | |
| Pass | 1♠ | Pass | 2♡ |
| Pass | 2♠ | Pass | 4♡ |
| All Pass | | | |

The deal comes from the 1998 Spingold tournament in the USA. At the other table Marcin Lesniewski and Marek Szymanowski also reached 4♡ against silent opponents and made eleven tricks after the helpful lead of the ◇A. Here, Cezary Balicki found the stronger lead of a club, choosing the ♣9 according to his methods. Declarer (whose name didn't make it to posterity) won with dummy's ace and spectacularly discarded the ♠A on the ♣K. He was then able to throw two diamonds on the ♠K and ♠Q.

Since the trumps were divided 3-2, declarer could have succeeded at this stage by playing on that suit. Not privy to such information, he tried a diamond to the king. Balicki won with the ace and cashed the ◇Q, drawing his partner's jack. Although the ◇10 and ◇9 were masters, Balicki led the ◇3, making it clear to his partner that he was looking for an uppercut. The diamond was ruffed in turn by dummy's ♡9, Adam Zmudsinki's ♡10 and South's ♡J. When declarer played the king of trumps, Balicki won the ace and conceded yet another ruff-and-discard in diamonds. Zmudzinski ruffed with the ♡8 and declarer had to overruff with the queen. Now West's ♡7 was promoted into the setting trick.

Was declarer wrong to play a diamond to the king, instead of drawing trumps? Not as we see it. Although a 3-2 trump break is more likely than finding the ◇A onside, declarer was by no means certain to encounter a trump promotion if a diamond to the king should lose.

If you weren't impressed by the last deal, let's see a modest six-spot being promoted. The deal is from the 1993 European Championships, contested in Menton, France:

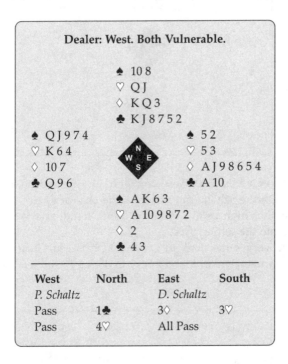

Dealer: West. Both Vulnerable.

|  | ♠ 10 8 |  |
|  | ♡ Q J |  |
|  | ◇ K Q 3 |  |
|  | ♣ K J 8 7 5 2 |  |

| ♠ Q J 9 7 4 | | ♠ 5 2 |
| ♡ K 6 4 | | ♡ 5 3 |
| ◇ 10 7 | | ◇ A J 9 8 6 5 4 |
| ♣ Q 9 6 | | ♣ A 10 |

|  | ♠ A K 6 3 |  |
|  | ♡ A 10 9 8 7 2 |  |
|  | ◇ 2 |  |
|  | ♣ 4 3 |  |

| West | North | East | South |
|------|-------|------|-------|
| *P. Schaltz* | | *D. Schaltz* | |
| Pass | 1♣ | 3◇ | 3♡ |
| Pass | 4♡ | All Pass | |

Peter Schaltz led the ◇10, covered by the king and the ace. His wife, Dorthe, returned a diamond to dummy's queen and declarer threw a club. The ♠A and ♠K were followed by a third spade, ruffed with dummy's ♡Q. When East showed out but could not overruff, the trump king could be placed with West. Needing to return to hand for a second spade ruff, declarer led the ◇3 and ruffed with the ace. Declarer scored a second spade ruff and once again had to find a route to his hand to draw trumps. The ♣K was taken by East's ace and declarer ruffed the diamond return with the ♡7, West throwing the ♣Q. These cards remained:

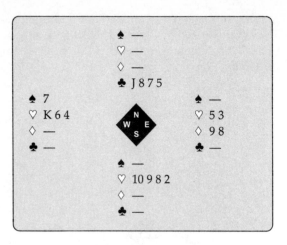

When declarer led the ♡10, West won with the king and led a fifth round of spades. Dorthe Schaltz did not miss the chance to ruff with her ♡5, forcing another high trump from the South hand, and West's ♡6 was promoted into the setting trick.

On the very same deal, in the match between Great Britain and Romania, Barnet Shenkin found a way to dodge the bullet. This was the bidding:

| West | North | East | South |
|------|-------|------|-------|
|      | *Steel* |    | *Shenkin* |
| Pass | 1♣ | 3◇ | Dbl |
| Pass | 3 NT | Pass | 4♡ |
| All Pass | | | |

West again led ◇10 to the king and ace and East returned the ◇4. Shenkin gave up the idea of ruffing both his spades, and concentrated instead on making an extra club trick. On the second diamond he threw a spade. He then ruffed his remaining spade loser and cleared trumps, conceding a trick to the king. In the end, he led a club to the jack to make his game.

In our previous examples, the trump to be promoted was accompanied by a higher-ranking one, like a corporal being protected by a colonel. How about a humble six being promoted when escorted only by a two-spot? It happened in the summer of 1998, in the Biarritz tournament:

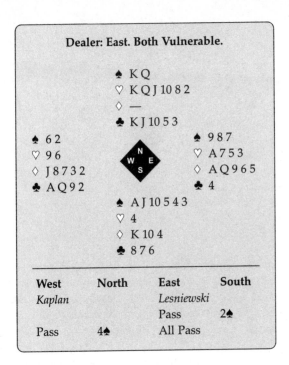

**Dealer: East. Both Vulnerable.**

|         | ♠ K Q            |         |
|         | ♡ K Q J 10 8 2   |         |
|         | ◇ —              |         |
|         | ♣ K J 10 5 3     |         |

| ♠ 6 2          |                  | ♠ 9 8 7          |
| ♡ 9 6          |                  | ♡ A 7 5 3        |
| ◇ J 8 7 3 2    |                  | ◇ A Q 9 6 5      |
| ♣ A Q 9 2      |                  | ♣ 4              |

|         | ♠ A J 10 5 4 3   |         |
|         | ♡ 4              |         |
|         | ◇ K 10 4         |         |
|         | ♣ 8 7 6          |         |

| West      | North   | East         | South   |
|-----------|---------|--------------|---------|
| *Kaplan*  |         | *Lesniewski* |         |
|           |         | Pass         | 2♠      |
| Pass      | 4♠      | All Pass     |         |

Lewis Kaplan led the ♡9 to his partner's ace and the singleton club was returned. Kaplan won with the ace and played back the ♣2. Suppose you had been the declarer would you have played the ♣K or the ♣J?

The club position was unclear, since if East held ♣Q-9-4 he could have placed West with the ♣A. In any case, declarer had a club discard available on dummy's hearts. After a long huddle, declarer put up the ♣K, ruffed by East. When the ◇A was returned, declarer ruffed with dummy's ♠Q and cashed a top heart, throwing his club loser. Knowing from the ♡9 lead that West was out of hearts, declarer played a third round of clubs. East ruffed with the ♠8, forcing declarer's ♠10, and declarer ruffed his losing diamond with dummy ♠K. This was the position:

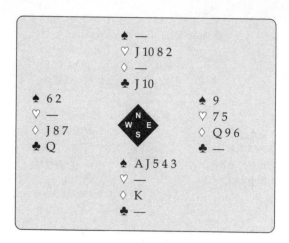

Declarer had no winning option. If he led a heart from dummy, this would immediately promote a trump trick for West. He tried the ♣J instead but East was there with his ♠9. This forced the ♠J from declarer and West's ♠6 was promoted into the setting trick. Could declarer have made the contract? Yes, but only by finessing the jack on the second round of clubs.

We're near the end of the chapter, so you will be expecting something a little more unusual. On the next deal both defenders benefited from a trump promotion. It comes from 2002 Danish Mixed Pairs Championship:

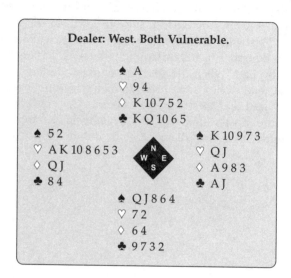

| West | North | East | South |
|------|-------|------|-------|
| 3♡ | Pass | 4♡ | Pass |
| Pass | 4NT | Dbl | 5♣ |
| Pass | Pass | Dbl | All Pass |

The usual score was 650 to East-West, for an overtrick in their heart game. At one table, North took the horrible view (particularly when holding a doubleton heart) to seek a good sacrifice in one of the minors. South ended in 5♣, doubled by East.

West began with a top heart, drawing the ♡Q from his partner. He does best to switch to the ◇Q next but at the table another top heart was cashed, followed by the ◇Q. Hoping that this card was a singleton, declarer erred by not covering. The ◇J then went to the king and ace. When a third round of diamonds was led, by East, declarer ruffed with the ♣9. This won the trick but West's ♣8 climbed one step higher up the ladder. When a trump was played to the king and ace, East was able to play another diamond and this time West overruffed South's ♣7 with the ♣8. A third round of hearts from West (delivering a ruff-and-discard, as in so many of the trump promotions that we have seen) then promoted East's ♣J. The defenders scored two hearts, two diamonds and no fewer than three trump tricks after the two-way promotion. A well-deserved +1400 their way.

We end the chapter with a curious deal. Again it comes from Denmark, from a 2001 tournament in Arhus. The defenders attempt a trump promotion at more than one table and there are three variations in the play:

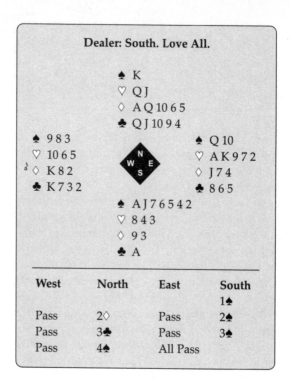

**Dealer: South. Love All.**

```
              ♠ K
              ♡ Q J
              ◇ A Q 10 6 5
              ♣ Q J 10 9 4
♠ 9 8 3                      ♠ Q 10
♡ 10 6 5        N            ♡ A K 9 7 2
◇ K 8 2      W     E         ◇ J 7 4
♣ K 7 3 2       S            ♣ 8 6 5
              ♠ A J 7 6 5 4 2
              ♡ 8 4 3
              ◇ 9 3
              ♣ A
```

| West | North | East | South |
|------|-------|------|-------|
|      |       |      | 1♠    |
| Pass | 2◇    | Pass | 2♠    |
| Pass | 3♣    | Pass | 3♠    |
| Pass | 4♠    | All Pass | |

At one table West led the ♡6, East cashing two hearts and playing a third round. The declarer, Danish international Steen Schou, ruffed with dummy's lone king, and then entered his hand with the ♣A to play ♠A and another. He encountered good luck and bad luck. East's queen appeared on the second round but ... a fourth round of hearts promoted West's ♠9 for down one.

Nothing mind-blowing so far but at another table, after the same start, Morten Stege sitting South refused to ruff the third round of hearts! He discarded a diamond from dummy, allowing West's ♡10 to win the trick. Thanks to the queen of trumps being doubleton and the ◇K being onside, he scored his game.

So, is the game always makeable? Not if the defenders are on their toes. At yet another table Morten Bilde led the ♡6 to his partner's king and then unblocked the ♡10 under the ace. When East played the ♡9 at Trick 3 it wouldn't help declarer to refuse to ruff in the dummy, since a fourth round of hearts from East would beat the contract. When he was congratulated for his fine unblocking play, West assumed a modest air. "We play middle-up-down!" he said.

# 29
# Turning Gold Into Stone

It's an even-money guess whether you will find this deal amusing or just plain silly. We're going to risk it, anyway. The scene is the 1996 Olympiad in Rhodes and the names of the players involved were not released to the general public. See who you would have blamed for the truly horrible bidding misunderstanding suffered by North-South:

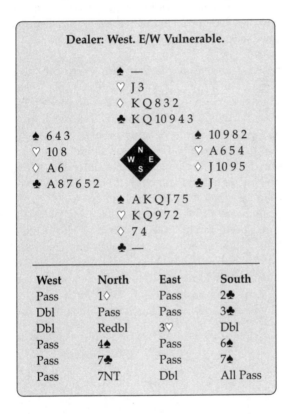

**Dealer: West. E/W Vulnerable.**

```
              ♠ —
              ♡ J 3
              ◇ K Q 8 3 2
              ♣ K Q 10 9 4 3
♠ 6 4 3                      ♠ 10 9 8 2
♡ 10 8              N         ♡ A 6 5 4
◇ A 6          W       E      ◇ J 10 9 5
♣ A 8 7 6 5 2       S         ♣ J
              ♠ A K Q J 7 5
              ♡ K Q 9 7 2
              ◇ 7 4
              ♣ —
```

| West | North | East | South |
|------|-------|------|-------|
| Pass | 1◇ | Pass | 2♣ |
| Dbl | Pass | Pass | 3♣ |
| Dbl | Redbl | 3♡ | Dbl |
| Pass | 4♠ | Pass | 6♠ |
| Pass | 7♣ | Pass | 7♠ |
| Pass | 7NT | Dbl | All Pass |

North-South were playing Precision, so North had to open 1◇ rather than 1♣. You might expect South to mention his spades at this stage but – no – his system dictated that he start with the artificial game-forcing response of 2♣. Since this did not show clubs, and North-South had already advertised the balance of the points, you would imagine that there was no doubt what West's double of 2♣ meant. It showed clubs. North passed now, although he might have redoubled to suggest playing in clubs. What would you have bid next on the South cards?

Simple souls that we are, we would say that there was no reason whatsoever not to introduce the spade suit at this stage. In the way that some players do, South resorted to science. He attempted to indicate a two-suiter in the unbid suits with a bid of 3♣! How should North interpret this, do you think? If South held a big club hand (which was possible only if West's first double had not in fact shown clubs), he would surely have passed 2♣ doubled. He would have been content with the score that a few doubled overtricks would bring in that contract. So, there was a sound case for saying that 3♣ was not a natural bid.

North's own splendid holding in clubs was further evidence that South's 3♣ could not be a natural bid. Just in case North still had some doubt on the matter, West persisted with a second penalty double. North, who had indeed taken 3♣ as natural, redoubled to show his enthusiasm for this contract.

East surely had no reason to say anything now but the auction had been confusing and he formed the view that his partner's original double of 1◇ – 2♣ might have been intended for take-out after all. He stepped in with 3♡ and South doubled. North had only to leave in this double and he would have picked up an enormous penalty. No, he was still under the impression that his side had a big club fit and in that case his hand was more suited to offence. He leapt to 4♠, intended as a splinter bid. South read the bid as natural, although it is hard to believe why North would have bid 4♠ rather than 3♠ if he held spades.

North-South were off the rails in a big way, with the train still running at full speed. South raised to 6♠ and North retreated to the 'known club fit', bidding 7♣. A puzzled South corrected into the 'known spade fit' and North then had nowhere to go but 7NT. The contract was doubled and declarer held his losses to the three aces, losing 500.

By pulling partner's double of 3♡, North had reversed the alchemist's dream. He had turned a golden +1700 into a stony -500.

# 30
# Sins Unpunished

In Chapter 21, we admired some brilliant plays that failed to pick up a swing because of unforeseen events at the other table. In this chapter we look at the converse phenomenon, where a grave error was committed and went unpunished. Sometimes the culprit even gained heavily, because some greater atrocity was committed against his team-mates.

Suppose you stop at the game level, missing a cold small slam – a possible grand slam, in fact – might you not expect to lose a bundle of IMPs, especially if you were playing a world championship? The Taipei East-West had a lucky escape on this deal, played against Venezuela in the 1987 Bermuda Bowl:

Dealer: North. East-West Vulnerable.

```
                    ♠ 10 5 4 3
                    ♡ A 10 3 2
                    ◇ K 3
                    ♣ 9 5 4
    ♠ Q 9 7                        ♠ A 6
    ♡ 7 6 5 4          N           ♡ —
    ◇ 9            W       E       ◇ A Q J 10 7 4
    ♣ A K 10 3 2       S           ♣ Q J 8 7 6
                    ♠ K J 8 2
                    ♡ K Q J 9 8
                    ◇ 8 6 5 2
                    ♣ —
```

| West | North | East | South |
|------|-------|------|-------|
| Kuo | Hamaoui | Shen | Caponi |
| | Pass | 1◇ | 1♡ |
| Pass | 2♡ | 3♣ | 3♡ |
| 4♡ | Pass | 5♣ | All Pass |

Che Kung Kuo did his best to catch up, when the massive club fit came to light. Chin Shan Shen had four big gaps in his hand, though, and it was difficult to imagine that a passed hand could plug three of them. This was particularly so if West's initial failure to bid was caused by substantial heart values. The Taipei players had no need to worry about the missed slam because this was auction at the other table:

| West | North | East | South |
|------|-------|------|-------|
| Onorati | Tai | Pasquini | Huang |
| | Pass | 1◇ | 1♡ |
| Pass | 2♡ | 3◇ | 3♡ |
| Dbl | All Pass | | |

East's 1◇ opening was Precision, which doesn't show many diamonds. Even so, it seems that he would have been better advised to rebid 3♣ instead of 3◇. Such a rebid would be compatible with the hand that he held, even if it might be based on a hand with longer clubs than diamonds.

What should West do over South's 3♡ bid? He may have thought that his double of 3♡ was competitive, but such an action is barely possible when he could not make a negative double of 1♡ on the first round. The second-round double is surely an out-and-out penalty double. East clearly took it as such, since he did not show his clubs even with a 6-5 shape. He must have read his partner for a trump stack.

The worst thing is that the Venezuelan defenders didn't even manage to beat 3♡ doubled. Declarer ruffed the ♣A lead and played a diamond to the king and ace. East continued with the ◇Q and ◇J, ruffed in the dummy. West, meanwhile, discarded two clubs. Declarer led a spade from dummy, rising successfully with the king. Now came the key moment – declarer led his last diamond and West had to play a card from ♠Q-9 ♡7-6-5-4 ♣K-10. Mario Onorati made the fatal decision to release a club, when a discard of the ♠9 (or a ruff) would have defeated the contract. Declarer ruffed in dummy and removed West's last club with a club ruff in hand. He then overtook the ♡K with the ♡A, leaving these cards still to be played:

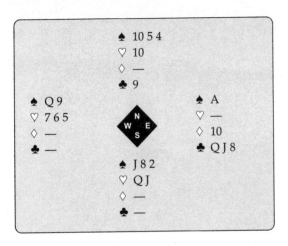

Declarer ruffed dummy's last club, West throwing the ♠9. When a spade was played to East's ace he had to return a minor-suit card and declarer was able to score his last trumps separately. It would not have helped East to throw the ♠A when declarer crossed to dummy with a trump, because West's retention of the ♠Q-9 would allow declarer to set up and enjoy a spade trick. So, the doubled contract of 3♡ was made and Taipei gained 15 IMPs, despite missing a cold slam at one table.

On the next deal, from the 1988 Olympiad in Venice, an American ladies pair played an icy grand slam in game and still managed to pick up a substantial swing. Thanks to the chivalry of the original reporter, no names are available:

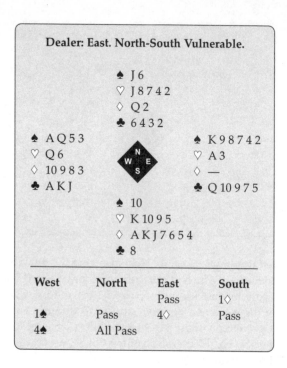

Dealer: East. North-South Vulnerable.

```
                    ♠ J 6
                    ♡ J 8 7 4 2
                    ◊ Q 2
                    ♣ 6 4 3 2
   ♠ A Q 5 3                      ♠ K 9 8 7 4 2
   ♡ Q 6              N           ♡ A 3
   ◊ 10 9 8 3     W     E         ◊ —
   ♣ A K J           S            ♣ Q 10 9 7 5
                    ♠ 10
                    ♡ K 10 9 5
                    ◊ A K J 7 6 5 4
                    ♣ 8
```

| West | North | East | South |
|------|-------|------|-------|
|      |       | Pass | 1◊ |
| 1♠ | Pass | 4◊ | Pass |
| 4♠ | All Pass | | |

Most players would open 1♠ on those East cards. The American East decided to pass, not a mistake, and her partner was then faced with a difficult call over South's 1◊ opening. Double, 1NT and 1♠ all have flaws. West chose 1♠ and drew an enthusiastic splinter-bid response from her partner. What next? The West hand had plenty going for it – a full 16 points for a one-level overcall and no points wasted in the splinter suit. Worried that she held only a four-card suit, she back-pedalled with a 4♠ rebid. East let matters rest there and thirteen tricks were easily made. The Americans must have feared a swing of at least 11 IMPs.

(Before we pass to events at the other table, note how foolish it would have been for South to double 4◊, as many players would. West would pass and East could then show that she had a void diamond by redoubling. A slam would surely have been reached.)

East-West fared even worse at the other table. Again let us apologise on behalf of the original reporter, who saw fit to provide no names. Imagine the newspaper report of a World Cup football match saying: "One of the Brazilian players then blasted the penalty kick wide of the left post".

| West | North | East | South |
|------|-------|------|-------|
|      |       | 2◊   | 3◊    |
| Dbl  | All Pass |   |       |

The Polish East did not overstate her splendid hand when she opened a humble Multi 2◊. Expecting that her partner's suit was hearts, West made the poor decision to double 3◊ (game was a near certainty their way, even if East's suit was hearts). The contract was cold. Declarer could even afford the luxury of playing hearts from her hand for two losers. So, the American pair who had played a grand slam in game, scored 510 at their table and 670 at the other, gaining 15 IMPs.

What next? You overcall on a ten-high suit of just four cards, get doubled in a 4-1 fit and go for 900. An expensive board? Yes, for the opponents! The deal arose in the 1984 Vanderbilt final:

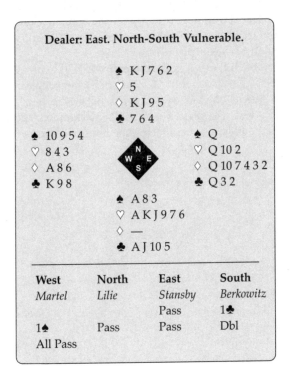

**Dealer: East. North-South Vulnerable.**

```
              ♠ K J 7 6 2
              ♡ 5
              ◊ K J 9 5
              ♣ 7 6 4
♠ 10 9 5 4                    ♠ Q
♡ 8 4 3                       ♡ Q 10 2
◊ A 8 6                       ◊ Q 10 7 4 3 2
♣ K 9 8                       ♣ Q 3 2
              ♠ A 8 3
              ♡ A K J 9 7 6
              ◊ —
              ♣ A J 10 5
```

| West | North | East | South |
|------|-------|------|-------|
| *Martel* | *Lilie* | *Stansby* | *Berkowitz* |
|      |       | Pass | 1♣ |
| 1♠   | Pass  | Pass | Dbl |
| All Pass |   |      |      |

David Berkowitz opened with a strong 1♣ and Chip Martel intervened with a light-hearted overcall (light-spaded, too, as Edgar Kaplan wrote in his report). Martel scored only two tricks. In those days the penalty was 900, rather than the 1100 it would have cost him today.

How on earth did Martel's indiscretion gain a heavy swing? Let's see the bidding at the other table:

| West | North | East | South |
|------|-------|------|-------|
| *Nagy* | *Pender* | *Levin* | *Ross* |
| | | 2♦ | Dbl |
| 5♦ | Dbl | Pass | 6♡ |
| All Pass | | | |

North-South were momentarily in a position to collect the same 900 from 5♦ doubled, thereby flattening the board. Expecting his partner's values to be spread more evenly across the suits, Hugh Ross tried his luck in 6♡. It was a poor contract, as you see, but the cards lay very fortunately. In fact, West can defeat the slam only if he leads the ♠5 or ♠4. Any other lead assists declarer in one or other of the tasks that he has to perform. Peter Nagy chose to lead a trump, picking up that suit, and declarer could then add five spade tricks and the club ace. That was +1430 and a pick-up of 11 IMPs for the 1♠ overcall at the other table.

As we approach the end of the chapter you will expect the hands to get more spectacular. How about Giorgio Belladonna gaining points by going seven down, playing in a cue-bid, when he had a cold slam available! The deal was played in a 1982 international tournament in Novara, with the Italian Juniors facing the mighty Lavazza team:

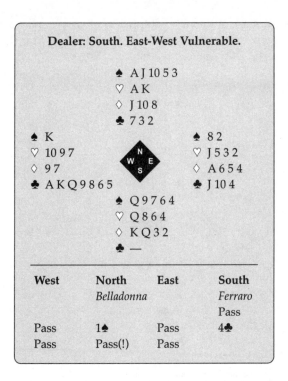

**Dealer: South. East-West Vulnerable.**

```
                    ♠ A J 10 5 3
                    ♡ A K
                    ◇ J 10 8
                    ♣ 7 3 2
    ♠ K                              ♠ 8 2
    ♡ 10 9 7            N            ♡ J 5 3 2
    ◇ 9 7           W     E          ◇ A 6 5 4
    ♣ A K Q 9 8 6 5     S            ♣ J 10 4
                    ♠ Q 9 7 6 4
                    ♡ Q 8 6 4
                    ◇ K Q 3 2
                    ♣ —
```

| West | North | East | South |
|------|-------|------|-------|
|      | *Belladonna* |  | *Ferraro* |
|      |       |      | Pass |
| Pass | 1♠ | Pass | 4♣ |
| Pass | Pass(!) | Pass | |

West's opening pass is astonishing but nothing like the later pass from Belladonna. He obviously had a blind spot, although he later complained to Guido Ferraro: "Can't you use simpler bidding?" The inglorious contract went seven down while a slam was available for North-South in spades. (It seems impossible to go more than five down in 4♣ so perhaps a disgruntled declarer committed a careless revoke.)

It was a champion of today, totally unknown in 1982, who saved the day for the Lavazza team. In the other room, Norberto Bocchi was West, partnering Arturo Franco. He opened the West hand with a gambling 3NT and scored nine tricks when the junior sitting North led the ♠J!

The text-book advice, when leading against a Gambling 3NT, is to lay down an ace in order to see the dummy. Had the Italian junior, sitting North, borne this in mind, his side would have scored five spades and three hearts, scoring +400. They would then have had quite a story to tell – putting the great Belladonna team seven down in one room and four down in the other. As it was, Lavazza gained 6 IMPs on the board. At half-time the great Belladonna seemed to discern some mirth among the juniors, albeit hidden behind the awe of playing against such a legend. "You have laughed enough," he told them, red in the face and furious with himself. "You are not going to score a single point more in this match." He was right. His team won the second half by 56 to 0!

Two internationals, in a long established partnership, play a cold small slam in a two-level part-score. Might they perhaps lose IMPs on the board? Let's see. The deal comes from the 2001 Bermuda Bowl in Paris:

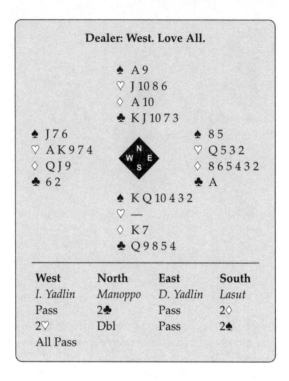

**Dealer: West. Love All.**

```
                    ♠ A 9
                    ♡ J 10 8 6
                    ◇ A 10
                    ♣ K J 10 7 3
 ♠ J 7 6                          ♠ 8 5
 ♡ A K 9 7 4          N           ♡ Q 5 3 2
 ◇ Q J 9         W         E      ◇ 8 6 5 4 3 2
 ♣ 6 2               S           ♣ A
                    ♠ K Q 10 4 3 2
                    ♡ —
                    ◇ K 7
                    ♣ Q 9 8 5 4
```

| West | North | East | South |
|------|-------|------|-------|
| *I. Yadlin* | *Manoppo* | *D. Yadlin* | *Lasut* |
| Pass | 2♣ | Pass | 2◇ |
| 2♡ | Dbl | Pass | 2♠ |
| All Pass | | | |

Manoppo opened with a natural Precision 2♣ opening. Henky Lasut's 2◇ response was not game-forcing but it was the usual first response on all strong hands, asking the opener to describe his hand further. When the Israeli West entered with 2♡, Manoppo doubled to show that he had a side suit of hearts. What should Lasut bid next?

He took the view that 2♠ would be forcing, because he could have responded 2♠ initially on a fairly weak hand with long spades. Manoppo did not share this interpretation and the Indonesians scored four overtricks in their inglorious partial.

Did the Israeli North-South pair reach a slam on the North-South cards? Surely it would be too difficult with only 23 points between the hands. Amazingly, they did reach a slam. Even more astonishingly, it was a grand slam! Manoppo and Lasut therefore won 7 IMPs for their bidding misunderstanding instead of losing 12, as they deserved. You would like to have seen how the Israelis reached the seven level? So would we! We are sad to tell you that our investigations ran into a wall of silence. The world will never know.

# 31
# Snap!

We end the book with a rare deal indeed. In a world championship final both teams bid to a grand slam when missing a cashable ace. What's more, they both made it! This is the deal, from the final of the 2000 Women's Team Olympiad in Maastricht, with USA facing Canada:

**Dealer: West. Both Vulnerable.**

```
                    ♠ J 7 6 5
                    ♡ A K Q J 8 5
                    ◇ —
                    ♣ K 9 7
     ♠ 8 3                         ♠ K 10 9 4
     ♡ 7 4 2           N           ♡ 10 9 3
     ◇ J 9 5      W         E      ◇ 10 2
     ♣ J 6 5 3 2       S           ♣ A Q 10 8
                    ♠ A Q 2
                    ♡ 6
                    ◇ A K Q 8 7 6 4 3
                    ♣ 4
```

| West | North | East | South |
|------|-------|------|-------|
| *Thorpe* | *Quinn* | *Gordon* | *Breed* |
| Pass | 1♡ | Pass | 2◇ |
| Pass | 3♡ | Pass | 4NT |
| Pass | 5♠ | Pass | 7NT |
| All Pass | | | |

Mildred Breed, for the USA, bid Roman Key-card Blackwood with hearts agreed. The response showed two key-cards and the trump queen. Her partner's jump rebid in hearts made it likely that North held ♡A-K-Q rather than the two missing aces and the ♡Q. Breed jumped to 7NT nevertheless (one report claimed that she had miscounted the missing key-cards. A low club lead would have beaten the grand by two tricks. A double-dummy ♣J lead would have beaten it by four tricks. No, West led a heart and when diamonds broke 3-2 declarer was able to claim the contract.

Is there any way that East might have attracted a club lead? Suppose she had doubled 7NT. What lead would that have suggested? East had already spurned the chance to double 5♠, so it is unlikely that she wanted a spade lead. The general consensus at the time is that a double would have asked for a heart lead, despite the use of RKCB in hearts.

Mildred Breed was doubtless hoping for a massive swing her way after such a large stroke of luck. However, this was the bidding at the other table, where the Canadians held the big hands:

| West | North | East | South |
|------|-------|------|-------|
| *Hamman* | *Lacroix* | *Sutherlin* | *Cimon* |
| Pass | 1♡ | Pass | 3♢ |
| Pass | 3♡ | Pass | 4♢ |
| Pass | 6♢ | Pass | 7♢ |
| All Pass | | | |

Francine Cimon's jump shift, followed by a rebid in the suit, showed solid diamonds. Martine Lacroix now jumped to a small slam in diamonds, not intending this bid to have any specific meaning in terms of side-suit controls. The Canadian South had to guess what her partner held. Taking the view that the 6♢ bid promised a fair number of controls, such as the ♠K, ♡A and ♣A, she raised to the grand slam. Petra Hamman led a trump and thirteen tricks were made. The Canadian North-South must have been disappointed indeed to lose 2 IMPs after this adventure.

Who do you blame for the Canadian auction, albeit a successful one as it turned out? North had a difficult bid over 4♢. She could visualize a huge number of tricks in the red suits but was lacking in black-suit controls. We don't think a leap to 6♢ was justified and would prefer a restrained 4♡, leaving space for South to bid Blackwood. If 4♡ is thought to be insufficient, a bolder 5♡ would show the source of tricks and suggest an alternative trump suit. That said, it is surely not right for South to place her partner with disparate controls in the black suits (♠K and ♣A) when she did leap to the six level. With such cards, facing an unlimited partner, it would be North's duty to cue-bid the ace that she held. So, as we see it, a jump to 6♢ rather suggested that North held second-round controls in both black suits.

An exhilarating deal, anyway, with the two North-South pairs playing in contracts that might have led to tears their way. No, they ended up laughing (not openly, one hopes) and the tears belonged to the opponents. Long may the game that we all love provide such drama!